Epiphanies of Darkness

CHARLES E. WINQUIST

Epiphanies of Darkness

Deconstruction in Theology

Philadelphia

Library of Congress Cataloging-in-Publication Data

Winquist, Charles E., 1944–
  Epiphanies of darkness.

  Bibliography: p.
  Includes index.
    1. Theology—Methodology.   2. Theology—20th century.
I. Title.
BR118.W59   1986   230'.01   85–45479
ISBN 0–8006–1903–X

2096J85   Printed in the United States of America   1-1903

For Joan Marie Amatucci

Contents

Preface

Behind all the European faiths, religious and political, we find the first chapter of Genesis, which tells us that the world was created properly, that human existence is good, and that we are therefore entitled to multiply. Let us call this basic faith a *categorical agreement with being.*
—Milan Kundera, *The Unbearable Lightness of Being*

And briefly, if you had thought more subtly, observed better, and learned more, you certainly would not go on calling this "duty" of yours and this "conscience" of yours duty and conscience. Your understanding *of the manner in which moral judgments have originated* would spoil these grand words for you, just as other grand words, like "sin" and "salvation of the soul" and "redemption" have been spoiled for you. — And now don't cite the categorical imperative, my friend! This term tickles my ear and makes me laugh despite your serious presence. It makes me think of the old Kant who had obtained the "thing in itself" *by stealth*—another very ridiculous thing!—and was punished for this when the "categorical imperative" crept stealthily into his heart and led him *astray*—back to "God," "soul," "freedom," and "immortality," like a fox who loses his way and goes astray back into his cage.
—Friedrich Nietzsche, *The Gay Science*

... Every revelation partook more of significant darkness than of explanatory light.
—Herman Melville, *Moby Dick*

The basic faith, the categorical agreement with being, was profoundly challenged by Immanuel Kant's first critique. But perhaps Friedrich Nietzsche was right: Kant lost his way and inadvertently wandered back into his cage. The transcendental critique of objective knowledge was an achievement from within a rational framework that undermined the possibilities for completeness in the western metaphysical and theological traditions. In the voice of Kant, rationalism

turned on itself and challenged its basic faith. Objective knowledge
cannot become absolute knowledge. Kant demarcated a domain of
otherness that is inaccessible to objective knowledge. Theology is left
without a proper *object* of study.

Attempts to overcome the enigma of consciousness that so profoundly marks the first Kantian critique have been hard to maintain
credibly through the passage of intellectual and political history. The
categorical imperative of Kant's moral philosophy, the realization of
the absolute spirit in Hegelian idealism, or a phenomenological science
that is also a teleology are not thinkable in the same way after the
insights of the great masters of suspicion, Marx, Nietzsche, and Freud.
Not only did they wound the metaphysical tradition with concepts
of ideology, the unconscious, and the will to power, but they also
supplemented a political history of abjection where the unthinkable
war to end all wars was followed by the unthinkable Holocaust and
all the other powers of horror that are now commonplace in
international political and economic life.

The problem of this book is not the Kantianism of the three
critiques, although I do think the *Critique of Pure Reason* challenges
the faith that Kundera calls a categorical agreement with being. My
question is how to understand the practice of theological thinking
after that faith has wavered. It would be hard to justify a theology
that is an ideological elaboration of a categorical agreement with
being if we have an intellectual conscience. The witness of history
should cause us to question the felicity of totalizing theological
projects that overlook our history of abjection and engender a basic
faith that the world was created properly.

The witness of the unthought and unthinkable showed itself in the
critical philosophies of the Enlightenment. But in light of Hegelian
idealism and its many offspring it was hard to imagine how much the
problem of the unthinkable was to be deepened by a series of
epiphanies—epiphanies of darkness. It is at the extremities of philosophical, psychoanalytic, and theological thinking that the excess of
the unthought is experienced as loss, lack, and desire. It is at these
extremities that we need to experiment with new modes of argumentation. Postmodern discourse will involve the recognition of
wounds in and to rational argumentation. It will refuse to understand
argument as a seamless fabric or linear progression. The concept of
argument is itself deconstructed by reading the tropes or turns in
language that characterize the discourse as levers of intervention. A
deconstructive theology is a tropology.

A theological tropology is different from traditional systematic theologies. Theology has always entertained unrestricted concepts that push us toward the root of our discursive domain. But in postmodern theologies that root will resemble less the taproot of systematic theologies supporting a tree of knowledge growing above the ground than a rhizome. A rhizome that matures underground becomes more substantial when its stems spread underground in starts, false starts, and blockages. The rhizome is elaboration in itself. Stems reach out that can intertwine with other stems. Lines stop/start, intersect, and we have different modalities for argument and thinking.

A Rhizome can be cracked and broken at any point; it starts off again following one or another of its lines, or even other lines.... Every rhizome includes lines of segmentation according to which it is stratified, territorialized, organized, signified ... but also lines of deterritorialization.... the line of flight is part of the rhizome.[1]

The self-understanding of a postmodern theology is constituted in a fluid succession of images. It is a nomadic discipline, a marginal discipline, an underground growth. Its strategy is not the completion of a system but the location of a dwelling that will give a home to our homelessness.

The ironic outcome of systems of totalization is an "unbearable lightness of being." The strategies of totalization are strategies of refusal that will not bear the return of the repressed. Nature and history are segregated and subsumed under totalizing systems; they confine people to a domain of abjection. This domain is outside the order of things. Totalizing theologies cannot speak from these margins but only about them. Nevertheless we bear a responsibility for marginal people and marginal ideas.

Therefore theology cannot at this time with intellectual conscience make a wager to bracket our knowledge of the epiphanies of darkness and reinstate the speculative and systematic enterprise.

So my proposal for theological understanding is experimental. It could become dadaism and that is a risk. But there is also a risk that we will wander inadvertently back into our cages. In some ways deconstruction in theology resembles a second-order critique looking for the conditions that make theological thinking possible. There is a difference, however.

The deconstructionist problem is the problem of text: we are in a text. Theological thinking is text production: the text is a supplement. We can't simply get outside, behind, or beneath the text. Critical intervention is from the inside and is better construed as transgressive rather than transcendental.

The work of interpretation is intervention that repeats rather than completes itself. This book works with strategies of repetition continually wandering into the margins of discourse in philosophy, psychoanalysis, and theology. The hope is that the epiphanies of darkness are a repetition of wounds that compel language to come near the human enigma.

NOTE

1. Gilles Deleuze and Felix Guattari, *On the Line* (New York: Semiotext(e), Inc., 1983), 17, 18.

Acknowledgments

"The Subversion and Transcendence of the Subject" first appeared in the *Journal of the American Academy of Religion* 48, no. 1 (March 1980) and is used with permission.

"The Epistemology of Darkness" originally appeared in the *Journal of the American Academy of Religion* 49, no. 1 (March 1981) and is used with permission.

Portions of this book appeared originally as "Thomas J. J. Altizer: In Retrospect" in *Religious Studies Review* 8, vol. 4 (1982), pp. 337–42 and are used by permission.

"The Archaeology of the Imagination: Preliminary Excavations" originally appeared in the *Journal of the American Academy of Religions Thematic Studies* 49, no. 2 (1982) and is used with permission.

"Body, Text and Imagination" from *Deconstruction and Theology* by Thomas J. J. Altizer, et al. Copyright © 1982 by The Crossroad Publishing Company. Reprinted by permission of The Crossroad Publishing Company.

"Metaphor and the Accession to Theological Language" originally appeared in the *Journal of the American Academy of Religion Thematic Studies* 49, no. 1 (1982) and is used with permission.

Portions of this book were originally published in *Zygon* 18, no. 3 (September 1983) and are used by permission.

1

The Subversion and Transcendence
of the Subject

"In a dark time, the eye begins to see ..." is the first line of a poem by Theodore Roethke that concludes by saying, "The mind enters itself, and God the mind, And one is One, free in the tearing wind."[1]

For many people this is a dark time, and the intrusion of God into the involution of thinking and seeing poses a dilemma for understanding. It is indeed a strange homecoming when the mind enters itself and discovers traces of forgotten and distant cultures, obscure images of God or gods, and perennial philosophical questions juxtaposed with the anticipated memories of a distant childhood. The intrusion of God and the psychological resonances with unfamiliar iconographies seem to be produced by the darkness that turns us inward. The distance between understanding and the depth of this strange psychological experience is further augmented by the cultural anomaly of lives in our midst and collective memory that are enriched by patterns of religious meaning.

It is not simply the biographies of saints, gurus, and prophets that are strangely distant from modern experience; there are also in our presence the anachronistic remnants of faithful individuals nurtured by the sacramental way of life,[2] daily devotion, puritan renunciation, and countless other spiritual disciplines. In addition to these dimly perceived faces that mirror religious depth is the increasing talk of holistic visions. These visions elude the theologians and philosophers that have accommodated themselves to the secular world by accepting into their purview that which is ordinary, clear, and distinct.

In 1969 Langdon Gilkey portrayed the theological ferment of that time as a movement "from the question of the character of God to the more radical question of his reality and from the question of the nature and forms of religious language to the more radical question

1

of its possibility as a mode of meaningful discourse."[3] He suggested that if the use of religious language is not a possible mode of meaningful discourse it is because the use of religious language is totally disrelated to experience and life.[4] Gilkey accurately described academic theology at that time, as is evidenced in the subsequent self-indulgence of theology in methodological questions. At that time it would have been reasonable to expect that if this radical crisis of meaning concerning the use of religious language was not speedily resolved, talk of God would soon disappear. No paradigmatic achievement in theological thinking gained widespread acceptance as a solution to this crisis, and yet this reasonable expectation was false.

The crisis has not been resolved. Talk of God, gods, and goddesses, the initiation of spiritual quests, the presence of spiritual charlatans, and the church-going public have endured this radical crisis of meaning. In fact, it appears the highly articulate theological reflections on religious language have had little impact on experience or life.

Academic theology is in a state of moribund suspension at present. Gilkey's description of the crisis in theology was, and is, an accurate description of the crisis of theology. It was talk about talk of God that was sensed to be totally unrelated to life and experience. The crisis was internal to theology, although it quickly extended throughout the whole domain of the study of religion. The loss of connectedness was between talk about religion on the one hand and religion on the other. God-talk and other religious uses of language continue to be given in our cultural experience. Meaning is already embodied in the discursive act. To question the possibility of religious discourse is properly a transcendental question that proceeds from the phenomenology of the experience. If the question of possibility becomes an object of inquiry beside the experience that is its object, then the emergent sense of crisis is primarily descriptive of the discipline and not of religion (the first object of its inquiry).

This does not mean, of course, that there is no crisis in religion or that modern human beings are not in search of a soul. It simply means that the delineation of the methodological crisis of meaning refers back to itself. The crisis has occurred because we experience a distance between our way of thinking and religious experience itself. We are frustrated by not being able to explicate thematically the anomalous quality of religious experience that resists extinction in an otherwise secular world.

The turn in theology from questions concerning the character of

God to the question of the existence of God does not tell us anything about God. What it does reveal is our own posture of alienation from the world of immediate and traditional religious experience. This radical inquiry clears the way for what has emerged as a hermeneutical problem.

The hermeneutical problem only emerges clearly when there is no powerful tradition present to absorb one's own attitude into itself and when one is aware of confronting an alien tradition to which he has never belonged or one he no longer unquestionably accepts.[5]

The achievement of much recent theology is a clear understanding of the distance between where it stands and muted meanings embodied in experience. The symptoms of a theological melancholia, the nostalgic memories of a lost object of desire, reveal a wound in the intellectual process, however, that may itself be a passage to deeper understanding. The ancient wisdom that "only the wounded physician can heal" may be applied to the contemporary theologian.

The resistance of religious experience to dissolution and its distance from understanding constitute the hermeneutical problem. We have realized that the inability to assign meaning to an experience is not identical with the claim that the experience has no significance. We must learn to respect that characteristic of the material that resists thematic articulation and to understand that the resistance is part of its significance. If a physician is not able accurately to diagnose an illness from the manifest symptoms, this does not mean that the symptoms are insignificant. It is of course always possible that the inability to understand the meaning of a particular experience is a reflection on the nature of the experience.

We skew the significance of experience if we seek clarity and distinctness where there is no clarity because of the ambivalent nature of the experience. This is particularly true if we identify clarification with simplification. I am not, however, suggesting that there are intrinsically unintelligible experiences—only that intelligibility sometimes requires a complexification of consciousness and an overdetermination in the play of meaning. Understanding can require an artful display of images in experiments that alter fundamental notions of self, reality, and importance. In other examples the systematic delineation of classical functional relationships brings intelligibility to experience. We might even see the applicability of statistical models in the determination of probable relational patterns. In whatever example we choose, intelligibility is a multivalent concept.

First there is the intrinsic intelligibility of the experience. The experience belongs to a nexus of relationships, and this pattern of connectedness is constitutive of the experience. When we say an experience is meaningless, seldom are we claiming that the experience is disconnected from everything else and stands in the metaphysical void. What we usually intend in such a claim is the confession that we are unable consciously to connect this experience with other experiences, or that familiar patterns of meaning cannot be applied literally to particular experience.

This reveals a second and more common notion of intelligibility. Thinking delineates an extended or secondary relationship to experience. The secondary relationship is a function of how we stand in relationship to primary experience. This definition of secondary intelligibility is confused by the fact that, in its own right, the act of thinking (i.e., establishing a secondary relationship) is a primary experience. Thus, it is always difficult to determine when we espouse a crisis of meaning whether we are referring to a relational deficiency or to our own inability to discern relationships in the linguistic transformation of the complex of events that are the original objects of thinking.

Since we cannot begin in any other place than where we are, even if our beginning is a movement away from the beginning, serious accounts of experience must respect the resistance of material at hand to being other than what it is. If we work without regard to how experience presents itself, we will be confronted with an intellectual analogue to what psychoanalysts have called the return of the repressed. The experience will remain untouched by our understanding and repeatedly manifest itself over against the intelligibility of the most rigorous philosophical and theological explanations.

In light of our secular expectations, the persistence of religious experience is a clear example of this return of the repressed. Thinking without regard to the resistance of religious phenomena to simple translation into a text of exclusively secular understanding is a flight from empiricism that characterizes the shape of a method but not the shape of religious experience. We become aware of what is excluded from the purview of an inquiry when it persists as an anomaly in relationship to the achievement of the discipline defined by its methodological principles. What is unique in much contemporary theology is that religious experience is anomalous to theology's world view. This strange state of affairs does not fault the integrity of secular theologians. In fact, the discovery that many of us live in the secular city and not in the city of God is an important insight for the study of religious experience. What is particularly interesting is that religion has persisted in the secular city.

The identification of religious experience with religious institutions in describing the religious situation is a simplistic misreading of religious experience that intertwines an institutional crisis with the intellectual crisis of contemporary theology. Certainly we cannot ignore the presence of institutions, but they are not the exclusive vessel for religious experience. The religious dimension of experience will not cease to be a matter of human interest regardless of the future of religious institutions.[6] We must carefully avoid the category mistake of confusing epiphenomena of religious experience with religious experience. Religious experiences constituted sacramentally through institutional life may exist and be increasingly disconnected from everyday life, but they too must now be assessed by how they present themselves in modern consciousness.

In this example the two characteristics of *survival* and *distance* are now part of the meaning of this experience. The discursive situation in which we talk about meaning is itself part of the significance of the present situation. It is the discursive situation that has been altered as the institution has been weakened as a major authority in defining the objects of religious understanding. The irregular dispersion of concepts throughout various historical epochs does not dissolve the nexus of primary connections that are operative in the persistence of religion. Discussion and analysis of the discursive situation is a delineation of the secondary relationship to primary experience. It is an account of our presence and therein lies its primary significance.

This discussion of primary/secondary relationships and the primary qualities of secondary relationships is intended to clarify what is necessarily a complex activity. We must not only accept responsibility for appropriately recognizing the overdetermination of meaning in the symbolic objects of religious studies, but also recognize that the process of inquiry is a multivalent activity. Religious experience in its originating situation is also connected to the discursive situations that admit it into the contemporary situation. The contemporary valences are primary and secondary, and there are meanings made determinate through discourses concerning both patterns of connection. The connections of the past are already meaningful relationships that are drawn into a discourse constituting new meanings also subject to analysis. Just as the past relationships reside in a multiplicity of patterns of discourse and can be analyzed sociologically, psychologically, historically, philosophically, and theologically, the new relationships are subject to multiple patterns of complementary interpretation.

One of the profound sources of dissatisfaction in contemporary theology is that we have not experienced the depth and density of the relationship that we have established. That is, we have not experienced the quality of our own experiencing; it is inarticulate and not thematically related to other prominent events in our lives. We have literalized the hermeneutical gap between the past and the present, and we then experience the distance between past constellations of events and our present complicity in the past as meaningless in regard to the past events. The whole enterprise is diminished in the self-consciousness of its importance.

The alternation between celebration and mourning in the radical theology of the sixties made it clear that there is something significant in the monuments of the religious past and that we have experienced our distance from that past. What was difficult to assess in the immediate moment of this recognition was the significance of where we were standing. In the courageous tradition of Luther many theologians could say, "Here I stand, I cannot do otherwise";[7] but, in distinction from Luther, the referent of *here* is an obscure experience of an ambivalent middle. Theology must experiment and become familiar with the meaning of the middle of experience, which is the beginning and where we still stand.

Inquiry in foundational theology revolves so much around the question of where we stand that it seems distant from both tradition and an active theology of proclamation. Theologies of proclamation seem strangely deficient in meaning because although they may be internally rich, they are not richly connected to our sense of the contemporary situation. Thomas J. J. Altizer has suggested recently that his purpose is "to open yet another way to a new theological language, a language that will be biblical and contemporary at once and altogether."[8] His grasp toward a new genre for theological thinking appears to be an experiment in primal thinking and is not easy to imitate. It does, however, suggest new directions for future inquiry. It is possible to experiment with genre in foundational inquiry as well as in a theology of proclamation. Because I do not know where we stand, my own inclination, in distinction to Altizer's experiment with a language of proclamation, is to turn to theories of discourse and there experiment with the primary meaning of the secondary relationship to religious phenomena. We can begin with a question as to whether there are multiple modalities for thinking, genres for discourse, that are already present (which is in the middle of experience). Is there more than one genre that can contain the turning of thought and language on itself? We need to make sense out of that "dark time" when "The mind enters itself, and God the mind."

The immediate problem we face when thinking turns inward and God is there is that we do not have an adequate conceptuality for rendering this experience intelligible. Pure epistemology is compromised by the theological exigency. Schubert Ogden has claimed that "the only way any conception of God can be made more than a mere idea having nothing to do with reality is to exhibit it as the most adequate reflective account we can give of certain experiences in which we all inescapably share." His further delineation of the problem complicates the situation. He maintains that "God is radically different from everything else we experience."[9] The problem is how can we give an adequate reflective account of experience that necessarily involves talk of God when "God" is used in discourse in radically different ways from everything else that we bring into language. *Our problem is not the absence of God but the presence and reality of the concept of God.* We have a place for God but hesitate before our talk of God. Foundational thinking in theology is immediately caught in the problem of God. It cannot assume an autonomous posture without falsifying and simplifying the complexity of experience. In a reflective mode, epistemology is complicated by theology, and theology does not have an adequate conceptuality for talking about God without rethinking its epistemological foundations. The obvious complication is that this process of rethinking cannot come to satisfaction without our being able to talk about God. In order to talk about God we need a deepened insight into insight—which itself requires talk about God. We must change our mode of thinking about thinking and our mode of talking about God if the middle of experience is to have any meaning for us. Since we have no other beginning without a falsification of experience, these questions are fundamental to both epistemology and theology.

Our continual focus on the complexity of the middle is intended to help us hold fast to the integrity of experience even when this requires that we consent to being cast adrift in ambiguity and confusion. The middle does not approximate a *tabula rasa* or resemble a clean, well-lighted place. It is reality already mediated by language and crowded with images that are overdetermined and multivalent. The clean, crisp questions of transcendental epistemology are quickly burdened by phenomenological descriptions that implicate us in the full range of psychological life. Theology accepts the burden of incarnate meaning when it begins its work from the middle. In contemporary theology we see evidence of this consent to embodied meaning in a variety of conceptual shifts.

For example, the appeal to process philosophy in Schubert Ogden's *The Reality of God* is oriented around Whitehead's reformed subjectivist principle. "The principle requires that we take as the experiential basis of all our most fundamental concepts the primal phenomenon of our own existence as experiencing subjects or selves."[10] This is a principle of inclusion. It refers to *all* our most fundamental concepts and the primal phenomenon of our own existence. "Nothing can be omitted, experience drunk and experience sober, experience sleeping and experience waking ... experience in the light and experience in the dark, experience normal and experience abnormal."[11] Ogden's appeal to Alfred North Whitehead for an adequate conceptuality to house both the depth of the Christian witness and the range of secular experience is a commitment to the embodiment of meaning. This beginning sacrifices the narcissistic satisfactions of theological abstraction for the relevance of all experience.

A parallel example, also radical in its claim, can be discovered in the philosophical and theological writings of Bernard Lonergan. He refuses to prescind from an analysis of subjectivity, intersubjectivity, and the subject's religious horizon. Everything that pertains to the subject in its context pertains to investigations in a philosophy of God. "This means that intellectual, moral and religious conversion have to be taken into account."[12] Thus, we are in the mediate realm of the middle.

Lonergan draws our attention to the experience of understanding, judging and deciding. We move away from the natural attitude in this account of ourselves. "Our attention is apt to be focused on the object, while our conscious operating remains peripheral. We must, then, enlarge our interest, recall that one and the same operation not only intends an object but also reveals an intending subject."[13] The intending subject is a complex notion. Intentionality implies an objective environment and opens the possibility for intersubjectivity. In particular, "meaning is embodied or carried in human intersubjectivity, in art, in symbols, in language, and in the lives and deeds of persons."[14] Our beginning is necessarily implicated in this full range of experience as it reveals an intending subject.

We can abstract the structure of intentionality from its connections in a world of meaning (which is itself a discursive situation). If we do this, we are then not talking about our experience of experiencing. An extended analysis limited exclusively to structural considerations leaves the scene of meaning too quickly and thereby sacrifices density for clarity. The pleasure of pneumatic flight, the lifting of the spirit in abstract thinking, finds its meaning only when it mirrors the grounding of the soul in the full body of experience. The connection must be made, because structural abstraction is not a substitute for the logic of the soul. We must learn to respect the linguistic, cultural, and psychological facts of the intending subject and include them in theoretical reflections.

The focus on the full context of the intending subject as a possible resolution of the crisis in contemporary theology clearly characterizes our situation as a crisis of being in the middle, a mid-life crisis. Although we have approached the mid-life situation as an epistemological-theological crisis, we quickly see that it can also be viewed as a psychological crisis. Part of our frustration in working through an epistemological solution is that there is a psychological remainder. Working out of the middle of life requires both psychological and epistemological insights—not a simple overlay of one on the other. A new genre is needed for thinking this way. The problems of a crisis of the middle in epistemology and psychology have a double reference. Both disciplines are related to it in their forms of interpretive discourse. The mid-life crisis is itself an overdetermined concept; we experience it in its duplicity.

We can start with either epistemological or psychological interpretations, and if we respect the resistance of experience to reduction, the concepts will be symbolically implicated in both disciplines. The questions raised by each discipline function heuristically and anticipate what is to be known in that discipline. The experience of the middle is shape-shifting as we alternate between the hovering attention of epistemological and psychological investigations. The questions of each discipline violate fixed expressions of horizontally determined meaning given in the language at our place of beginning. We discover possibilities that transcend the organizational patterns to which ordinary experiences have been conformed in ordinary discourse.

These questions come out of the middle and challenge the adequacy of the resolution that is also identified as the middle. Each discipline describes a rift in the world of ordinary experience that is a problem for an affirmation of the middling concept of a whole person.

There are actually numerous problems that question the demand to begin in the middle. If there were any other starting point that did not falsify experience, I would suggest that we reorient our inquiry there. But we do not have this choice, because even such a choice would be from the middle. We turned to epistemology to explore talk about God because talk of God persists in the middle of experience, and it is our beginning in the middle that we seek to understand. We quickly discover, however, that talk of God is also a problem for epistemologically reflecting the intending subject with its radical possibilities for asking questions. We also acknowledge that our inquiry is further complicated by psychological connections made determinate in the discourse about experience.

If we temporarily bracket radical concepts such as the unconscious (or other psychological connections that subvert discourse in the middle of experience), we still confront a hermeneutical problem. A naive sense of conscious activity can suggest an epistemological aporia. In fact, the complicity of theology with epistemology in the ambiguity of middle experience is already an expression of what could be described as epistemological or theological aporetics. We discover a connection or passage between these two dimensions of inquiry that is necessary but impassable without a prior resolution of meaning to which we can appeal. Such a prior resolution of meaning is demanded by the range of conscious activity but is not accessible to consciousness because it constitutes a transcendence of consciousness. In the middle, we experience the self as transcending but not the self as transcended.[15]

Thus epistemology begins to deconstruct itself. The basic concept of the subject is confused. For example, it is obvious that the subject transcends exclusive subjectivity by the very fact that it intends an object. The act transcends the subject even if the object is profanely ordinary, although it also includes the subject and thus transcends the content of exclusively objective expression of consciousness. We experience an immediate distancing of the content of unconsciousness from the conscious act and the lack of containment of the subject in the object or the object in the subject. The transformation of knowing action into conscious content is always an abstraction that is also an alienation from the fullness of experience. Subjectivity is the penumbral shadow surrounding the clear light of objective consciousness. It is never experienced as the pure act of consciousness but becomes obliquely available as a condition for what has already appeared as given in the objective pole of experience. The subject persists in questions that are formally transcendent, such as "what makes objective knowledge possible?" Amidst such familiar epistemological problems, the subject is manifested as a condition and not as an object of experience. We might say that the recurrence of such questions is the symptomatic presence of the subject.

The force of the transcendental questioning reveals the darkness that surrounds objective experience and places the subject in that darkness. An epistemology that approximates the experience of experiencing is an epistemology of darkness. This insight is both a symptom and a symbol of reflection on the light.

The symptomatic meaning of the subject can be extended by increasing the range and force of questions. Its day in discourse is unlimited. That is, through questions the subject can be implicated in all experiences and covers the world. In this way the surface of experience is subverted by the symptomatic appearance of the subject. Even the appearance of the subject as object is challenged by the presence of the subject as a condition and not as an object of reflective consciousness.

The appearance of the subject can be schematically pictured as a vertical intersection in a horizontal pattern of object relationships. This vertical image of the presence of the subject is akin to concepts of the human spirit. It is a spiritual improvisation on the substance of ordinary meaning that approximates a transmutation of flesh into spirit. That is, the world veils a transcendence apprehensible in the presentment of the subject that transcends the experience bringing it into view.

In this sense, transcendental epistemology can be thought of as an explicit pneumatic intrusion into the natural attitude toward experience and its expression in ordinary discourse. It makes explicit a transcendence that is a wound to our understanding. We can then radicalize the subject by ever increasing the range of its significance in experience. There is no self-contained discipline for thinking, because no boundary is immune from limiting questions of what lies beyond its demarcation. The questions are unrestricted, the intention is unrestricted, and the self in its subjective aspect is presented as an unrestricted desire to know. Here the subject is not given as an object. It remains shrouded in mystery, and consent to the subject is an acknowledgment of a mystery even in the midst of our most ordinary experience.

Thematic explication of the subject can only approach the meaning of the subject. It is not a descriptive exercise but a metaphorical invocation of meaning. Its fundamental purpose is disclosure or representation of the subject accompanying all conscious experience. Epistemology, particularly in its service of theology, generates experience of experience and is a self-conscious duplication in language of the transcending subject. Because of the transcendence of the subject, its achievement cannot be more than approximate. This discloses an unrealized realm for further connectedness that trespasses the boundaries of rational thinking. Our work always locates itself in a surplus of meaning that is paradoxically experienced as a wound to consciousness or gap in intelligibility. Neither theology nor transcendental epistemology can come to closure.

The designation of the transcending subject as a manifestation of the human spirit, *pneuma*, in distinction to the soul, *psyche*, is an attempt to respect divergent imaginal presentations of the order of the nonrealized. The vertical rupture of the horizontal plane of ordinary experience is expressed in dipolar images. That is, images of the transcendence of the subject can be contrasted to images of the complex unconscious web of individual and collective histories. The presentment of the transcending subject represents a significant rupture of the ordinary, as does the constellation of archetypal forces speaking from the common soil of our human and animal histories. The flight of the spirit and the archaeology of the soul equally challenge the complacency of our adjustments to the middle of life.

Of course, this distinction between psychic and pneumatic images is heuristic. The realities of experience these images designate are not neatly catalogued and separated. They share the characteristic of revealing themselves in the dark gap we experience as an intellectual aporia. This experience of distance gives weight to the hermeneutical problem and is not delimited within either the psychological or the theological field. The forgetfulness we experience as absence is a forgetfulness of spirit and soul.

Consent to the transcending subject parallels in importance the discovery of the unconscious in depth psychologies. Both discoveries point to realms in the discursive determination of meaning that represent a dispossession of consciousness as the sole place and origin of meaning. Depth psychology points toward a text of the primitive speech of desire as a complement to the explicit texts of manifest dream content and the pathological voices of neurosis, psychosis, and other aberrations of ordinary experience. "To interpret is to displace the origin of meaning to another region."[16] Foundational theology points toward the disclosure of possibilities for the sublation of the texts of ordinary experience into those extraordinary texts that might be called the *verbum* of the hierophanies. In depth psychology there is a dispossession of consciousness as the place and origin of meaning[17] through the discovery of the unconscious. In foundational theology the discovery of the transcending subject is of parallel significance and is also a dispossession of consciousness manifest in the rupture of the text. In both examples the surface of experience and the pretensions of rational intelligibility are subverted by seeing through fissures in ordinary texts to possible orders of meaning that are not realized in familiar patterns of conscious thinking.

The theater of ordinary experience may be glimpsed as middle-life situated between a semantics of desire and the verbum of the hierophanies. This duplex expression of what lingers in disguise behind the scripts of everyday life is an abstract formulation for what is concretely experienced as crises of disorder, disruption, and darkness. The subversion and transcendence of the subject are intruders that are symptomatically expressed as maladjustment in the dark calm of familiar experience. Whether it be in the rest-less-ness of our shared condition of quiet desperation or in the cacophony of mad voices, when we carefully gather our experiences of life in the middle, we are witnesses to a surplus of meaning that is at once a hope and a problem. Once again, our problem is that when the mind enters itself, God (gods, goddesses, and other extraordinary determinants of meaning) enters the mind. Paradoxically, we often do not know how to receive this rich inheritance and instead experience it as a dispossession of the prerogatives of ordinary thinking.

Part of the reason we do not know how to receive this meaning into ordinary thinking is that we experience as extraordinary the solicitation of the subject by possible meanings that are not within its established domain. We have no familiar tools to facilitate passage into this realm of possible meanings, and consequently experience

the call as the disclosure of an aporia. Thus, the revealing of a surplus
of meaning can be experienced as a frustration. This should not be a
surprise. Traditionally, when an experience reveals something other
than itself, it becomes taboo and therefore unavailable. "The elements
of the taboo itself are always the same: certain things, or persons, or
places belong in some way to a different order of being and therefore
any contact with them will produce an upheaval at the ontological
level which might well prove fatal."[18] Not only the originating
experience, but also the symbol that is rooted in the experience, is
able to carry on the process of hierophanization[19] and can produce
an upheaval. The traditional taboo is seldom articulated in modern
experience as a specific taboo. It is more frequently expressed by the
resistance to the presence of uncanny feelings and symptoms of
discomfort. The taboo or symptoms of disease are protective of the
claims of ordinary consciousness because the concept of the transcendence of the subject is as threatening to ordinary thinking as the
subversion of the subject in the discovery of the unconscious. Both
are a displacement of the subject and delimit the power of consciousness in the determination of meaning.

The verbum of the hierophanies can be defined as the inner word
produced by the disclosure of an order of meaning that is not realized.
In this sense we are talking about a text of extraordinary meaning,
and when it is a *text* of experience we can begin to appreciate its
function and status in relationship to the conscious determination of
meaning. The distinction between the act and content of conscious
intentionality is particularly important in the assessment of extraordinary meaning. The transcending subject is not what is known but
is a contextual process that is both a way of experience and an
experience in itself. The transcending subject touches and can be
touched. That it is more than what can be known is what is meant
by the transcendence of the subject. What is not known is, of course,
indeterminate and signifies an order of the nonrealized.

What is remarkable about the verbum of the hierophanies is that
tradition has witnessed to its autonomy in relationship to the subject
in much the same way that we acknowledge the disruption of expected
meanings by the presentment of the unconscious in psychopathology.
That is, when an event reveals itself as overdetermined we experience
an impulse toward realms of meaning that extend beyond the control
of intentional consciousness. Consciousness is initially displaced by
its lack of control and can appropriate the experience only by learning
how to stand in relationship to it.

The autonomy of the verbum alters our conception of language and our notion of the subject. We are drawn to a voice behind language that is itself language. Or, as suggested by Heidegger, in this experience "language itself brings itself to language."[20] That is, language is allowed to speak and this meaning of "to say" is "to show, to make appear, the lighting-concealing-releasing offer of world."[21] The meanings of our subjectivity and existence itself are altered by our being brought into the neighborhood of the nonrealized. Or, as Heidegger would say, the saying that is calling "brings the presence of what was previously uncalled into a nearness."[22] The "experience we undergo with language will touch the innermost nexus of our existence."[23] The transcending subject is now implicated in the power of language, and the meaning of the transcendent subject is determined as much by the signifying power of the text as by the intentionality of the conscious act. The transcendent subject is necessarily an overdetermined reality.

The displacement of the function of conscious decision as the sole arbiter of meaning through a rethinking of language is not new with Heidegger. The doctrine of *sola scriptura* is a hermeneutic thesis at the heart of Reformation theology that challenges the expectations of ordinary thinking as much as the doctrine *sola fides* challenges the prerogatives of common attitudes toward morality and good works. Gerhard Ebeling interprets this qualification of the word of God to mean that "the primary phenomenon in the realm of understanding is not understanding *of* language, but understanding *through* language."[24] Thus, "in dealing with a text there is a transition from an exposition *of* the text to an exposition *by* the text."[25] The text transcends the subject, yet is determinative of experience that reveals the subject. This possibility is opened by recognition of the mystery of what we have already called the transcendence of the subject. The interpretive power of the text resides in the calling of nonrealized possibilities into the proximity of the concept of the subject, thereby reconstituting both the showing of the world and the meaning of the subject that emerges as a correlate of conscious intentionality. The text, the subject, and the world are implicated in a drama of ambivalence that is "lighting-concealing-releasing." The disclosure of the subject is now also an announcement that there remains a hiddenness of meaning because the subject is revealed in its connectedness to the power of the text and the meaning of the world. The realization of the subject is the realization of an order of meaning that must remain not fully determinate in the content of understanding.

What we can understand is that there is a natural aporia signified by the transcendence of the subject. Thus, there is a natural darkness.

The darkness of the time is an image of disorientation. It is a time when God enters the mind: the God of Abraham, Isaac, and Jacob or perhaps the mask of Dionysus.

The image of a dark time has an ambiguous reference. It does not explicitly reveal which God has entered the mind. We do not know which forces or meanings have uprooted the security of conscious identity in common texts. It could be that we have described an act of faith known to the hearers of the word of God where "faith is security where no security can be seen ... the readiness to enter confidently into the darkness of the future."[26] The dark time is then a time of solicitation by the force of what we have called the verbum of the hierophanies. The image is here a signifier of the transcendence of the subject. The empirical ego is no longer congruent with its foundation in the subject. The other possibility to which we have frequently referred is that the dark time is an image for the subversion of the subject by the presence of dynamic unconscious forces.

The transcendence and subversion of the subject presents itself in the ambiguity of mixed discourse. In both instances the signifier belongs to the semantics of meaning and is determinate in this realm. It is the subversion of meaning that moves us into the realm of instinctual forces.

Because the unconscious is structured as a language is structured[27] and the verbum of the hierophanies is the inner capacity to receive revelation as a language, language is a subtle body for *psyche* and *pneuma*. Lacan's claim that "the unconscious is that part of the concrete discourse, insofar as it is transindividual, that is, not at the disposal of the subject in re-establishing the continuity of his conscious discourse"[28] can also be a claim of foundational theology as it describes the sublation of the text of ordinary experience into the transindividual texts of religious discourse.

The problem with the vertical intrusions of the various orders of the nonrealized is that we do not know what realm of discourse has inserted its claim through the wound in consciousness. The lure toward an expansive pattern of new meanings eludes the grasp of conventional language. We can only clearly acknowledge that we are in the middle of experience and that it is a dark time. We must learn either to think in the dark or to think darkly if we are to discursively integrate what is already our experience. The needed epistemology of darkness is not so much a theory of knowledge as an experiment with the depth and density of meanings within thought and discourse.

NOTES

1. Theodore Roethke, *The Collected Poems* (Garden City, N.Y.: Doubleday & Co., 1961), 239.

2. Edward Schillebeeckx, *Christ the Sacrament of the Encounter with God* (New York: Sheed & Ward, 1963), 221.

3. Langdon Gilkey, *Naming the Whirlwind: The Renewal of God-Language* (Indianapolis: Bobbs-Merrill, 1969), 13.

4. Ibid., 18.

5. Hans-Georg Gadamer, *Philosophical Hermeneutics* (Berkeley: University of California Press, 1976), 46.

6. Louis Dupre, *The Other Dimension: A Search for the Meaning of Religious Attitudes* (Garden City, N.Y.: Doubleday & Co., 1972), 5.

7. Roland H. Bainton, *Here I Stand: A Life of Martin Luther* (Nashville: Abingdon-Cokesbury Press, 1950), 186.

8. Thomas J. J. Altizer, *The Self-Embodiment of God* (New York: Harper & Row, 1977), 6.

9. Schubert Ogden, *The Reality of God* (New York: Harper & Row, 1963), 20-21.

10. Ibid., 57.

11. Alfred North Whitehead, *Adventures of Ideas* (New York: The New American Library, 1933), 227.

12. Bernard J. F. Lonergan, *Philosophy of God, and Theology* (Philadelphia: Westminster Press, 1973), 13.

13. Bernard J. F. Lonergan, *Method in Theology* (New York: Herder & Herder, 1975), 15.

14. Ibid., 57.

15. Ibid., 15.

16. Paul Ricoeur, *Freud and Philosophy: An Essay on Interpretation* (New Haven: Yale Univ. Press, 1970), 91.

17. Ibid., 494.

18. Mircea Eliade, *Patterns in Comparative Religion* (Cleveland: World Publishing Co., 1963), 17.

19. Ibid., 447.

20. Martin Heidegger, *On the Way Toward Language* (New York: Harper & Row, 1971), 59.

21. Ibid., 107.

22. Martin Heidegger, *Poetry, Language, Thought* (New York: Harper Colophon Books, 1975), 198.

23. Heidegger, *On the Way Toward Language*, 57.

24. Gerhard Ebeling, *Word and Faith* (Philadelphia: Fortress Press, 1966), 318.

25. Gerhard Ebeling, *Theology and Proclamation* (Philadelphia: Fortress Press, 1966), 28.

26. Rudolf Bultmann, *Jesus Christ and Mythology* (New York: Charles Scribner's Sons, 1958), 40–41.

27. Jacques Lacan, *The Four Fundamental Concepts of Psycho-Analysis* (New York: W. W. Norton, 1978), 20.

28. Jacques Lacan, *Écrits: A Selection* (New York: W. W. Norton, 1977), 49.

2

The Epistemology
of Darkness

... we do not mourn that we see through a glass darkly, we now rejoice
in the dark loveliness of the glass.[1]

—John Dominic Crossan

The theologian after the death of God, the end of philosophy, and
the end of theology is left with a critical vocation in a postcritical
age. The call to discernment, separation, and judgment about claims
from the history of theology amidst the persistence of religious
experience is complicated by the attraction of planting at least one
foot firmly on the soil of ordinary language usage. The quick and
uneasy alliance with the social sciences, the preemptive rise of secular
studies in religion, and the delimitation of the range of theological
inquiry by positivistic philosophies have not dispelled the surplus of
unsaid meaning calling from the darkness of primary religious experience. This oxymoronic state of affairs is a conceptual impertinence
that is itself a trace of a forgotten moment of originating consciousness.
The unsaid, the unconscious, and the order of the nonrealized name
the memory trace that reminds the theologian of both the subversion
and the transcendence of the subject.

When the reflections of ordinary language philosophies become
paradigmatic for the study of religion, the growing residue of unintelligible confessions becomes for theology an inheritance of the
unsaid. The semantic anxiety in the face of the unsaid has frequently
led to a delimitation of the tasks of theology and the study of religion.
The inclination is then to dismiss arrogantly or to mourn the fate of
those who continue to see through a glass darkly.

To "rejoice in the dark loveliness of the glass" is an alteration of
values that suggests we can know the darkness, think in the dark, or

think darkly. The concept of the epistemology of darkness is an experiment with this suggestion. Paradoxically, we are seeking to illumine the possibility for thinking darkly.

Learning to see in the dark is learning to bring darkness to the light; that is, learning to see the light darkly. We are now at the heart of an epistemology of darkness that acknowledges that part of language that "has a completely unfathomable unconsciousness of itself."[2] Can the darkness of language work on the transformation of consciousness? We cannot decide in advance of the experience whether it is possible and what it means to move the familiar and habitual world into the context of the imaginal world.

The task at hand is to replicate the familiar world of daily life in the shadow world of the imagination. The world we already know can then be known in the dark. We thereby teach ourselves to think in the dark so that we can live in the middle. This strange exercise is a taking hold of life. It is a valuation of where and who we are. It is a conjunction of thinking and feeling if the feeling function is understood as a differentiation of value. The whole process is a *work* within a semantics of meaning and is a function of consciousness.

The most immediately available paradigm for seeing the light and familiar darkly is the common experience of dreaming. Dreams take daily life into the underworld, and the *dream-work* is exemplary of downward thinking.[3] In the investigation of what it means to see darkly, it is not the interpretation of dreams but the interpretation of the dream-work that will be the primary path toward understanding. This work will be a hermeneutics of the second order. We are interpreting a process that is itself a process of interpretation. That is, the dream-work is an interpretation of the waking world that blurs the focus of a monocular vision and drowns the clear ring of univocal speech in a cacophony of metaphorical voices. The meaning of the manifest dream content is a psychological enigma and the meaning of the dream-work is an epistemological enigma. Analysis of dream content and analysis of dream-work are both interpretations of a secondary order, and both of them are distinguishable from the primary interpretation that is identified as the dream-work.

The specific concept of dream-work is one of Freud's great contributions to a psychology of the imagination. By developing a purely psychical apparatus he allowed for the meaningfulness of the dream images apart from neurophysiological explanation. Psyche was liberated and valued for itself.

In Freud's understanding the reason for this liberation belongs to the dark history of desire, but we can first examine his description of the dream-work without evaluating the superstructure of his meta-psychology. Our interest is with the strangeness of the dream.

When Herbert Silberer wrote an introductory summary of Freud's understanding of dreams, he reviewed the four principles that direct dream-work: condensation, displacement, representability, and secondary elaboration. He also said that "a part of the dream thoughts (not all) belongs regularly to the titanic elements of the psyche."[4] Then, after a lengthy and remarkable display of his own interpretive skills, Silberer makes the intriguing suggestion that "the point is to seize the wildly rushing spirits and to get possession of the powers without injury."[5] The question we are inclined to ask is: "How does the dream-work get possession of the powers without injury?" If dream-work is akin to seeing darkly, the answer to this question is an important advance through the dark passage of imaginal thinking.

The four principles help us focus our inquiry. Freud begins with condensation because "the first thing that becomes clear to anyone who compares the dream content with the dream thoughts is that a work of *condensation* on a large scale has been carried out."[6] The images in the manifest dream content are overdetermined. That is, the image is connected with many dream thoughts. It is multivalent or has multiple references within the world of daily experience.

One of the most easily understood examples of condensation is the construction of collective and composite figures.[7] The collective figure refers to each of its separate ingredients but is not any one of them. The image is a nexus of relationships. "New unities are formed and ... intermediate common entities are constructed."[8] Another clear example of condensation is the neologistic handling of words and names. Words and names are joined in composite expressions. Thus, the condensed images are pictorial and verbal.

The more difficult example of condensation is when associated patterns collapse and coagulate in a single image. In the examples Freud uses in his *Interpretation of Dreams,* the associations that are collapsed usually appear to be connected narratively. That is, the coagulation in the image is a collapse of temporal connections. What happened before and after is now simultaneously expressed in the dream image. Condensation ignores or abrogates temporal limitations. This does not imply that dreams do not have narrative forms in their expression. It simply means that the overdetermination of the dream image sometimes gives it an ahistorical signification. In this way, it might be suggested that condensation images eternity. With the dissolution and coagulation of the temporal determinants, the dream image has a vertical instead of a horizontal reference. The movement through the image is upward or downward.

The second principle Freud discusses is displacement. The *purpose* of displacement, which is a condition for the presence of a dream thought in the dream content, is as important for understanding this principle as the *mechanisms* he described. Before a dream thought can be an element in the dream content, it "must escape the censorship imposed by resistance."[9] The principle of displacement conjures up the mercurial image of the trickster delivering a message through duplicity and disguise.

The transference and displacement of psychical intensities discussed by Freud is a shift in value and importance among the latent dream thoughts. The dream becomes a recentering of waking life. The mechanism for this activity is the overdetermination of meaning in a specific image. That is, "overdetermination creates from elements of low psychical value new values."[10] Highly constellated psychic images slip into the theater of consciousness, and with the addition of this new material consciousness is itself displaced or recentered. The axis of experience is mobile and relative to the field in which it is determined.

From the description I have just given of Freud's understanding of condensation and displacement, it appears that they are comparable to rhetorical procedures and are a work of language. As Ricoeur points out in his study of Freud, this is only part of what Freud means by these principles. The concept of overdetermination is itself overdetermined because it is cast in realms of force and meaning. Ricoeur clearly recognizes this complication as a problem for Freud but also as a remarkable achievement of depth in his understanding. "This overdetermination, stated in the language of meanings, is the counterpart of processes stated in the language of forces."[11] He later refers to this understanding of the dream-work as a confusion of relations and says (surprisingly): "This jumbling of the infra- and the supra-linguistic is perhaps the most notable language achievement of the Freudian unconscious."[12] Ricoeur is, in the above quotation, referring to both the processes of condensation and displacement as well as the process or mobilization of stereotyped symbolization.

This takes us into the third and fourth principles: representability and secondary elaboration or revision. In the discussion of these principles, a deep epistemological problem emerges that cannot be reconciled within the framework in which the principles are developed. All these concepts are overdetermined such that they are connected to the epistemologically disjunctive realms of force and meaning. That is, we cannot know the realm of force as force but only as it is implied or represented in the realm of meaning. This would not appear to be such a great problem except that the dream-work process carries thought into the realm of force, and each of the guiding principles is implicated there. Thus our discussion of meaning is symptomatically elliptical. We begin to wonder whether the dream-work is just something that happens to us or if we can use it as a model of thinking darkly.

The third principle, representation, can be actively described as formal regression or a "forced substitution of one mode of expression for another."[13] The pictorial image is substituted for verbal expression in the construction of the dream content. This is a consideration of representability. "A thing that is pictorial is capable of being represented." More importantly, "concrete terms are richer in associations than conceptual ones."[14] Concrete terms are capable of being represented pictorially.

We can now begin to see how the third principle fits with the first two characteristics of the dream-work. If representability is to be a consideration in downward thinking, then what is admitted into this dark conscious content are terms rich in associations. Figuration or pictorialization is a process of overdetermination. What has hidden access to consciousness through this process of representation is a forbidden associative connection, but an equally important implication is that all the other associations to this representation also are connected to the dream content. The representation cannot be undone or deciphered by isolating only one of its associations without a loss of meaning. Like a work of art, the representation has its own status as a conjunctive achievement and cannot be returned or reduced to the artist's intention to discover its *true* meaning. Overdetermination is an achievement of complexity and, in representation, meaning dwells in that complexity.

The consideration of representability is a condition rather than a process in the dream-work. The active processes are condensation and displacement. There are, however, images from waking life that are already overdetermined. These images are symbols, and Freud acknowledges their significance in the formation of manifest dream content. "This ambiguity of symbols links up with the characteristic of dreams for admitting of 'overinterpretation'—for representing in a single piece of content thoughts and wishes which are often widely divergent in their nature."[15] Freud also thinks that symbolism is auxiliary because the work (overdetermination and displacement) has been done somewhere else than in the dream-work proper. He hesitates before the pregiven connections in the symbol;[16] but they are admitted into the dream-work because of the principle of representability. The symbol is a Trojan horse that could not be kept outside the boundaries of psychoanalytic theory.

Secondary revision or elaboration at first appears dissimilar from the other three principles. It seems to answer the demand of waking life for intelligibility and order. "It fills up the gaps in the dream-structure with shreds and patches. As a result of its efforts, the dream loses its appearance of absurdity and disconnectedness and approximates to the model of an intelligible experience."[17] Freud sees the purpose of this activity as fooling the censor. Elaborating or revising the material of the night-dream so that it looks like the wandering fantasy of a day-dream aims at reducing the importance of what has been produced through the dream-work. For example, within the dream there is sometimes the acknowledgment that "it is *only* a dream." The interpolations of censorship cast the dream in a matrix of "as though" or "as if " philosophies.

The intention of secondary elaboration may be, as Freud suggests, to disguise the importance of entertaining overdetermined images in consciousness; but secondary elaboration is also part of the process of overdetermination. One of the voices of the image refers to the world of waking life and the given patterns of connection to which it belongs in the waking world. It is the unique function of the overdetermined image and symbol to connect these semantically determined patterns of the waking world with the psychic forces of the underworld. Historical connections of the image are no less constitutive of the symbolic function than is an imaginal display of possibilities elaborated mythologically. By maintaining the fourth principle we are not able to sever from our consideration the importance of consciousness in understanding the dream-world. We are always talking about conscious experience. Even the discussion of unconscious determinants follows the path of what has been determined in manifestations of consciousness. Thinking darkly will be an achievement of consciousness.

Secondary revision is the preparation of the dream for reception into waking life. Freud quotes Havelock Ellis in the *Interpretation of Dreams* to illustrate this function. "Here comes our master, Waking Consciousness ... Quick! gather things up, put them in order—any order will do—before he enters to take possession."[18] The secondary revision is at the threshold of the passage between waking and dreaming consciousness. Since we are using the model of the dreamwork to experiment with thinking or seeing darkly, we will seek to cross this threshold not into the daylight but into the darkness. We have simply reversed the intentionality of the procedure.

Freud made a distinction between the revision that prepared the dream to cross the threshold into waking life and the content that belongs to the awareness of the threshold itself. He refers to Herbert Silberer's notion of the "functional phenomenon" to clarify this difference. The functional phenomenon is "the representation of a state rather than an object."[19] Freud viewed the correlate appearance of threshold symbolism as less important than the work of secondary revision. I have pointed out this distinction because in our discussion of thinking darkly it will be helpful to distinguish between carrying the ordinary world across the threshold into the darkness and the revisions that occur in relating to the images as overdetermined.

Thinking darkly begins with recognizable experiences, tangible feelings, and active fantasies. With an attitude of "evenly hovering attention" we collect these memories, experiences, feelings, and fantasies into the vivid immediacy of consciousness. There will be gaps, delays, and discontinuities that wound the surface and open the way for descent. Some of the surface images will resist the collecting processes of consciousness because they are rooted below the surface. Names are forgotten. Memories are incomplete. Associations are lost or skewed by a slip of the tongue or pen. The slips reveal their importance by their resistance to conscious display. Consciousness hesitates. It is not the sole arbiter of meaning even on the surface, which is the realm of its familiar and habitual control.

Consciousness can do more than note its hesitation reflectively. Through the structure of the question, it can reach into the darkness and incorporate meanings that it has not mastered. Hans-Georg Gadamer refers to this power to see what is questionable as hermeneutical consciousness.[20] The question comes to stand in consciousness as a presentment of indeterminate possibility. The form of the question is a structure for consent to the darkness of what is unknown.

Questioning attends to what resists articulation through configurations of the actual. The potentiality of its range is unlimited because there is no boundary that cannot itself be called into question. Because of this range, the temptation is to move too fast in a magnification of the possible and forget the beginning that is the middle. To experiment with thinking darkly, consciousness must seize the vertical structure of the question and direct it toward the soil of common human experience and on into the underworld. The pneumatic qualities of hermeneutical consciousness are thereby turned toward incarnation in the subtle body of psyche.

Directly correlated with Freud's discussion of secondary revision is the ability of consciousness to play before its watchful eye a stream of fantasies qualified by a suspension of judgment that provisionally withholds evaluation of their ontological status. They can be entertained in consciousness "as though" or "as if" they were important or unimportant. The reason for this procedure is to allow the image a place for display. The images are gathered in the process of collection and can then be incorporated into the downward thrust of the question as long as they are allowed to manifest themselves on the surface. The "as if" condition is also a suspension of external judgment. We can disguise thinking with the "as if" qualification so it appears that experience can be rehearsed without consequences. (In the dream-work this is a ploy to fool censorship.) The importance of the image is disguised so that it can reveal itself to consciousness. The temporary dissolution of external accountability does not cut off the image from its roots. Depotentiating external judgment by the qualification of "as if" does nothing to deny the image its symbolic voice. Secondary revision can be successful because surface consciousness guards its flanks and follows the horizontal line of semantic connectedness but is innocent of knowledge of the access through its depths.

In the same sense that secondary revision is a preparation for a dream to become conscious, there is a conscious preparation for thinking darkly. Consciousness functions at the beginning of this movement but will also function in a parallel fashion to the dream-work as a re-vision. The other three principles—condensation, displacement, and representation—can function simultaneously and elude any specific temporal sequence.

The conscious connection becomes more fragile as we follow the dream-work model into the shadow of overdetermination. There is a subtle interplay between the thinking and feeling functions of con-

sciousness. There is a need for value discrimination. When separating
its friends from its enemies, consciousness must subordinate the usual
alliance of light with the thinking function and befriend the darkness.
If the thinking function is dominant (a common occurrence in
academic and professional life), it must be displaced by assertion of
the feeling function in the priority of a value decision. What occurs
in this displacement is a transference of psychical intensities on a
conscious level. This is a close approximation of the meaning of
displacement in our understanding of dream-work. Not only is there
a shift in value, but also the importance of the valuational function
moves to the foreground.

In dream-work, one of the functions of displacement is to fool the
censor. On a conscious level we must choose not to censor our
thoughts or choose to fool the censor by admitting disguise into our
experience.

The first of these options is formulated in the famous fundamental
rule of psychoanalytic treatment: the patient should say everything
that comes into consciousness whatever the cost. The psychoanalytic
rule demands "the exclusion of all criticism of the unconscious or of
its derivatives."[21] This commitment to total communication is a valuing
of the connectedness that has not been brought into consciousness.
The actual procedure of free association races ahead of reflective
consciousness disclosing connections and images before it can be
ascertained they will threaten the provisional order already established
by consciousness in the flow of discourse.

The displacement and recentering of values on the conscious level
is also the necessary preparation for the second of the options:
representation or formal regression. Freud defines representation as
the forced substitution of one mode of expression for another.
Considerations of representability shift the direction of conscious
intentionality toward concrete terms that can be imaged. The substitution of one mode of expression for another is a process of
overdetermination. Each mode of expression is implicated in a
relational pattern that defines it as a mode of expression. The object
of thought gains connectedness through substitution of modes of
expression. A new consciousness dwells *in potentia* as possible
contrasts multiply in the shifting relational patterns given consciousness in new modes of expressivity.

Formal regression can become an exercise. We can choose to shift
modes of expression without foreknowledge of what new connections

will make this action significant. Painting, sculpture, waking dreams, and other activities of imaginal elaboration alter the texture of consciousness and overdetermine the meaning of the thinking that has been drawn into a substitute mode of expression. The gain in connectedness and overdetermination of the image do not necessarily issue in a new privilege of consciousness. There may actually be a dimming of consciousness because there are no readily available forms to conjoin and contrast the diverse patterns of connection generated in this activity. Formal regression darkens and complexifies the matter of experience. The ground of experience is enriched in preparation for cultivation.

Representability implies the admission of symbols into thinking. The conscious preparation is the displacement that ascertains the value of considerations for representability. Once the symbols are valued and thereby admitted into discourse, they speak their multiple voices and are not under conscious control. In a discussion of myth, James Hillman is very sensitive to the autonomous power of the symbolic function once it is admitted into consciousness through a mythological vessel. "No matter who deals with myth and no matter how unimaginative the approach, the imaginal world is struck and it echoes what is being said. We cannot touch myth without it touching us."[22] Although Hillman is not explicitly talking about the symbolic function here, we can gain an awareness of the risk and excitement of the power of the imaginal world as symbols are admitted into thinking.

Thinking darkly dwells in a realm of symbols and overdetermined meanings.[23] This realm is not identical with a world of metaphor, although to see this world may be an achievement of metaphorical thinking. The symbol is not just a coincidence of meanings. "Symbols have roots. Symbols plunge us into the shadowy experience of power."[24] Sacred mountains are subject to geological and imaginal history. The alchemist's "work against nature" presupposes nature, and therein lies the most difficult enigma for an epistemology of symbolic thinking—a thinking darkly. "The concept 'symbol' brings together two dimensions, we might even say, two universes of discourse, one linguistic and the other of a nonlinguistic order."[25] This duality is further complicated by overdetermination, or a multiplicity of connections, internal to each of the realms of discourse. The concept of a nonlinguistic order can be thematized within semantical discourse, but this is not the same as thematizing the nonlinguistic order. The dark forces remain dark.

The role consciousness plays in approximating condensation or overdetermination at first appears to be its opposite—overinterpretation. We have already seen, however, how representation and displacement can be approximated in conscious action and contribute to processes of overdetermination. When we examine overinterpretation, we have to remember that this work gives its product over to these other processes. Overinterpretation is a complex process, and in its first movement, the violence of foundational questions, it can directly contribute to condensation or overdetermination. Foundational questions yoke the actuality of the physical realm with images of possible connections that surround language and define its place in the material and imaginal worlds. Questioning loosens experience by asking how experience looks against a different background, under an expanded horizon, or when integrated through different formal patterns. The display of formal possibilities alters consciousness by generating contrasts between the semantic construction of immediate experience and what could have been or can be. Questions can lead to new juxtapositions of images that reverse and even eliminate temporal sequence. The resultant nontemporal condensations are images that speak new meanings.

The analogy we have established with Freud's dream-work requires a final move. When we mentioned secondary revision as a preparation for crossing the threshold, we realized the threshold would have to be crossed again so that we could present the dream-work to consciousness. The experience of seeing darkly or thinking darkly does not extinguish the meaning of consciousness, just as the dream's significance is established through the presentation of the dream-content in consciousness.

The conscious correlate to the process of secondary revision is the process of re-collection of experience that has been implicated in the overdetermination of meaning. Condensation, displacement, and formal regression have altered the middle of experience. Consciousness itself has been altered in two ways. First, in the displacement or recentering, the shift in value implies an openness to the complexity of the overdetermined image and symbol. The doorway into consciousness is made much broader. Second, the foundations of consciousness have been enlarged with contrasting configurations of the archetypal and the familiar. Consciousness has entertained the familiar with symbols derived from archetypal stories of religious and mythological history. The conjunction of the actual and the possible produces new configurations of the imaginal that are analogous to images in manifest dream-content. We can summarize our work, bringing that which is light into the dark, as a complexification of the familiar through the overdetermination of meaning. The actual images that manifest themselves as the issue of this process may be very simple. The complexification is a conjunctive elaboration of contrast at the foundations of consciousness.

The re-collection is not simply a repeat of the first collection of the familiar world. It is a cultivation of the richness of ground that has been prepared by seeing the light darkly. It is a re-vision. We are seeing the familiar against a background of archetypal situations or, stated more exactly, thinking in a context of archetypal configurations. This is not an allegorical interpretation that shifts the context of thinking away from the middle. Through the overdetermination of images, the archetypal figures have entered into direct commerce with the familiar figures of middle life. Their presence is intertwined with the darkness of language where middle life manifests itself.

The most telling characteristic of seeing or thinking darkly is that it takes place in the present. It is a consent to the middle. It is not the contrast with future possibilities that engenders the new consciousness, but the contrasts that are housed in the overdetermined images of the middle. This consciousness contains future referents but does not depend on the concept of the future for illumination. It is the mixture of the actual and possible that creates contrasts and engenders the dark consciousness of the middle. It is the shadow of truth that has been integrated into our vision. There is an intertwining of personal and archetypal meanings and there is a consciousness that is constituted in this configuration. When it is present we have learned to think darkly. Thinking darkly intends a configuration that when fully overdetermined is theological.

NOTES

1. John Dominic Crossan, *The Dark Interval: Toward a Theology of Story* (Niles, Ill.: Argus Communications, 1975), 39.

2. Hans-Georg Gadamer, *Philosophical Hermeneutics* (Berkeley: Univ. of California Press, 1976), 62.

3. Cf. James Hillman, "The Dream and the Underworld," *Eranos-Jahrbuch* (Leiden: E. J. Brill, 1975), vol. 42.

4. Herbert Silberer, *Hidden Symbolism of Alchemy and the Occult Arts* (New York: Dover Publications, 1971), 31.

5. Ibid., 321.

6. Sigmund Freud, *The Interpretation of Dreams* (New York: Avon Books, Discus Edition, 1965), 311–12.

7. Sigmund Freud, *Therapy and Technique* (New York: Collier Books, 1963), 328.

8. Freud, *Interpretation of Dreams*, 330.

9. Ibid., 344.

10. Ibid., 343.

11. Paul Ricoeur, *Freud and Philosophy: An Essay on Interpretation* (New Haven: Yale Univ. Press, 1970), 93–94.

12. Ibid., 405.

13. Ibid., 96.

14. Freud, *Interpretation of Dreams*, 375.

15. Ibid., 388–89.

16. Ricoeur, *Freud and Philosophy*, 102.

17. Freud, *Interpretation of Dreams*, 528.

18. Ibid., 539.

19. Ibid., 542.

20. Gadamer, *Philosophical Hermeneutics*, 13.

21. Freud, *Therapy and Technique*, 125.

22. James Hillman, *Pan and the Nightmare* (Zürich: Spring Publications, 1972), viii.

23. Ricoeur, *Freud and Philosophy*, 8.

24. Paul Ricoeur, *Interpretation Theory* (Fort Worth, Tex.: TCU Press, 1976), 69.

25. Ibid., 53–54.

3

The Archaeology of the Imagination

But we do not believe that madness has ever left us. Like pain it lies in wait for us at each stage, I mean each time we run up against the word hidden in the word, the being buried in the being.[1]

—Edmund Jabès

... it is madness which takes its original nature from the dream and reveals in this kinship that it is a liberation of the image in the dark night of reality.[2]

—Michel Foucault

There exists a desire to ground theological thinking in a philosophy of first principles that are themselves clear and distinct. The diminishing population of theological concepts outside the immediate focus of first principles suggests that the place to continue our investigation of possibilities for theological reflection is in an archaeology of knowledge. If we return to first principles we can then orient the adventure of theological thinking toward new paths of understanding.

This orientation to first principles has traditionally been the self-assigned task of foundational theology. The history of theology is replete with exemplary expressions of radical intentions followed by rigorous extensions and explanations of first principles. Plato, Aristotle, Descartes, Kant, Hegel, and Wittgenstein have guided legendary excavations into the ground of first principles that have been used as root metaphors in the construction of theological worlds. Foundational theologies have traditionally wrested from root metaphors principles for the expansion of meaning that could permeate ordinary experience. The work of theology has usually been thought of as a hermeneutics of expansion weaving a web of meaningful connections and saying what can be said about the relationship of common events and foundational principles. What could not be said, the surplus of meaning in even the most rationalistic theologies, fell into spaces of silence within and between systems and thereby constituted a presence that is an absence, a mystery and shadow for theological understanding.

If we are to initiate a new excavation, it must choose as its terrain the silences of experience, those suspicious areas of unintelligibility that have haunted the theological achievements of past enlightenments. The silences are those anomalous moments of experience of which rational thinking fails to speak. In this realm it is not the first principles but the silences that impress us with their forceful and vivacious presence. The desire to penetrate to foundations exists here no less than in a rationalistic theology, but the roots we now seek lie beyond or below principles that delimit the field of rational discourse. We realize that whenever we direct light on anything substantial it will cast a shadow, and that the shadow portends a reality that is no less real than what has been illuminated. The shadow is a gap or space that gives a new meaning to the old God of the gaps that cannot be exhausted by further achievements of rational understanding. Perhaps it was phenomenology or radical empiricisms with their tenacious holds on the full range of experience (including the vagaries of madness, dreams, and fantasies) that have forced on us a hermeneutic of suspicion via the precursor figures of Freud, Nietzsche, and Marx. It became difficult to look at the text of modern experience without suspecting that there was always a word hidden in the word. The hidden word becomes the sought-for treasure in a post-Enlightenment archaeological investigation. The heliotropic metaphor in its many familiar manifestations is made relative by the epistemology of darkness.

An archaeology that goes behind the rational to the neutrality of the image is based on the acknowledgment that the surface of experience cannot be described adequately by following the contours of rational explanation. Disrupted, distorted, and dazzled reason silences the sober judgments of ideal rationality. The persistence of the irrational points to a more complex epistemological whole behind conscious contrasts that is best represented through the approximation of images. This whole is always a metaphoric possibility.

The image stands prior to the differentiation between the rational and irrational. For rational thought there is an innocence of the imagination that exists prior to judgments of value or reality.[3] It would appear that the image waits for the decisions of rational thought to become a meaningful presence in the experience of the world. It is this appearance that leads us to think that the primal scene of thinking itself is the denomination of the world, the naming of the trees and animals, and that an archaeology of knowledge is a critique of reason. Even without benefit of the critical apparatus of a metaphysical system, the image assumes the ontological status of a given not dissimilar from the Platonic *eidos*. The image stands as a precritical intrusion in what are otherwise critical philosophies.

There are countless examples of the presence of images unfettered by the judgment of a reality principle. Primary narcissism, dreams, and "madness" all bear witness to valuation of images that present themselves independent of rational constraints. It is the rational constraint that marks the devaluation of the image as given and uncontrolled. As Michel Foucault has stated in *Madness and Civilization,* insanity as we know it is a product of the age of reason, a mirror image of rationality. Descartes' rigorous doubt that is almost at once a doubt of doubt does not hesitate very long before the dream-images or suspicions of madness evoked in the "First Meditation." The *Cogito* is the foundation of a certainty that quickly restores the world and God and also leads to the apodictic certainty of Kant. In like manner, Hegel's highway of despair is self-negated in a display of absolute spirit that shifts our attention from the ever-present "ship of fools" (a metaphor that has haunted Western thinking since the fifteenth century). An archaeology that too quickly assumes the form of a teleology is usually a critique of reason that is already committed to the light-metaphors of rationality.

Philosophies that remain untarnished by the vagaries of experience are never entirely convincing, even though they may be appealing. The dark nights of reality that house the shadows of the imagination are too much part of our historical and personal consciousness to adopt a rationalism that is more than nihilism. It is, however, not only the shadow of the imagination but the imagination itself that deserves our critical attention. The critical investigation that we have called an archaeology needs first of all to be an archaeology of the imagination.

The archaeology of the imagination can never begin at the origin we are seeking. The voice that directs our inquiry participates in a language and is bound to a language that is already sedimented. We discover that we seek new meanings in a realm that is governed by rules of syntax. No matter how the investigation is defined, its achievement will be linguistic and within a semantics of meaning.

Although it may appear obvious, this insight in itself touches on the fundamental problem for an epistemology of darkness. When the silences of the unsaid become said within a semantics of meaning, they are no longer themselves.

The problem is to understand the oxymoronic state of affairs at the very heart of our being-in-the-world. There is a hinge between the unsaid and the said, economics and semantics, force and meaning, that is by its nature necessarily a disjunctive conjunction. The dissimilarity of the realms of force and meaning conjoin at what must be the ontological equivalent to metaphor. This trope in the order of being is at the origin of our experience of consciousness; and because it is always there when we are conscious, we can only speak metaphorically of the origin of mind. The question of truth is lodged in the adequacy of our metaphorical thought. To think metaphorically is to experience a movement. "The point is not to listen to a series of propositions, but rather to follow the movement of showing."[4]

The archaeology of the imagination must start with the presence of images, and it is important to note that the image is simply present. It is our beginning and it is all we have. The image's presence reveals the absence of what it does not contain. We become aware of the absence through the re-presentation that is the presence of the image. A literalism of the imagination can give us only the image. Literalisms disguised as realisms portraying an objective world efface the presence of the image by the presumption that the relationship of image to image, a fundamental abstraction, signifies the image's presence. The presence of the image loses its meaning and mystery as attention is shifted to the possible play of connections between images. What is forgotten is the origin of the images, and this is the fundamental question for understanding the imagination.

An archaeology of the imagination searches for the origins of images as they constitute the first meaning of consciousness. The primal scene of origination is usually a diachronic fantasy that doubles the imagination by imagining imagination. It complements and informs an essentially synchronic foundational analysis. The fantasy informs foundational analysis by a reinforcement of what is given.

In the fantasy of a primal scene, a hyperbolic presence is given that is analogous with and sometimes identical to dreams and madness. Logocentric simplicity is disoriented by the liberated images, and the contours of experience to which foundational thinking addresses itself increase in complexity. The task has been made more difficult.

Rationality is superseded by the imagination. What is given exists prior to the judgment of rational or irrational.

The primal scene in diachronic fantasy is an unconscious elaboration of consent to the metaphorical basis of mind in foundational analysis. The consent can be experienced first as a humbling resignation that what appears to be the power of consciousness depends on a repression of the absent. Presence announces an absence that can be forgotten in the fascination with the interconnection of present images. But this absence can be likened to a word hidden in the word, a surplus of meaning, that subverts and transcends the fixed achievements of thinking.

Rekindled interest in Freud's notion of a primal scene is a witness to the power of imagination over fact.[5] It is also the plunging of the persistent mind/body dualism into the solvent of the imagination. This solvent of deconstruction is the primary agent of transformation in the rethinking of first principles in the reconstruction of epistemology.

When I refer to mind/body dualism I do not mean a specific philosophical theory that posits such a separation. I am referring to the problem of representation. How does the reality of the unsaid, whether we call it the unconscious, forgotten traces of Being, the economics of force, the order of the unrealized or even the body, present itself within a semantics of meaning? The simplistic affirmation of monism is a double disguise, the secondary repression of a primary repression. The absence announced by the presence of the signifier is an issue for all expressions of thought and not the peculiar problem of philosophies that espouse dualism. I am not referring to the content of a philosophical position but to the problem of the fundamental conjunction between dissimilar realms of connectedness. The evidence is extensive that there is a problem to be addressed.

Here we confront the other dimension (or dimension of the other) that is announced by speech and crystallized by writing. In theology we enter into this dilemma through a focus on the centrality of word-events. The unsaid is presumed in a saying that is both an affirmation and a self-negation. "The unsaid and the unsayable are truly the 'other' of speech, they are that which speech ceases to be when it is spoken. Once speech speaks it not only ceases to be unsaid, it becomes itself its own negation of the unsaid."[6] What we have defined is an aporia, an impassable passage. Our only access to the unsaid is the said, and the said can never itself be the unsaid.

The central problem can be clarified by looking at its statements in two precursor figures to contemporary deconstructionist thought: Heidegger and Freud. Parallels should not be confused with identities, but we must also not neglect the similarities among what at first appear to be dissimilar problems. Heidegger's insights and expression of the fall through the forgetfulness of language acts draws our attention to the ontological importance of the problem. As early as *Being and Time*, when he turned to a phenomenology to "let us see," we realized that what is present is not the theme that holds our interest.

> Manifestly, it is something that proximally and for the most part does not show itself at all: it is something that lies hidden, in contrast to that which proximally and for the most part does show itself, and it belongs to it so essentially as to constitute its meaning and its ground.[7]

The expressions of the disjunction between the ontic and the ontological that populate Heidegger's early work are conceptual images that both state the problem and turn our thinking toward the hidden voice of language.

The paradox in Heidegger is that the withholding of language is also a disclosure. In a later work he restates the problem:

> There is some evidence that the essential nature of language flatly refuses to express itself in words—in the language, that is, in which we make statements about language. If language everywhere withholds its nature in this sense, then such withholding is in the very nature of language.[8]

The paradox is that "the being of language is the language of being." We are brought into the neighborhood of Being, the silence of the unsaid, through the speaking of language; but it is not what language speaks that holds our attention if we release ourselves before its voice. Speaking in its most profound sense is a forgetfulness that is also an acknowledgment of that forgetfulness.

Where do we discover this speaking? Jacques Derrida suggests that the speaking that best contains this acknowledgment is a writing. Derrida and Heidegger both look for the language that is prior to language. Derrida's arche-writing and Heidegger's appeal to poetry assign a place for the diachronic fantasy of a primal scene. We are not talking about a common speaking or a common writing. ". . . Poetry never takes language as raw material ready to hand, rather it is poetry that first makes language possible."[9] We increasingly see that the primal scene is a demarcation of the extraordinary meaning of language. The sought-for first principles in an archaeology of the imagination appear to be poetic and metaphorical.

The scene of origination witnesses to forgetfulness or repression and begets mysticism or madness if we view its extraordinary qualities from the natural attitude of ordinary thinking. We are called to experience our conscious experience so that it is self-alienated. In this sense, consciousness is dispossessed by its achievement.

Heidegger is not the only witness to a scene of forgetfulness. There is also a psychological witness to this scene of origination: Freud is allied with Heidegger as this other witness to the force of the unsaid. Although he speaks in a psychological idiom, we are still confronted by a crisis in rational epistemology. The idiomatic difference between Freud and Heidegger in the expression of the epistemological problem does not detract from the force of what they say but instead points up a general problem for all thinking. The ontic characteristics of Freud's description of an economics of force cave in as the forces retreat from meaning and sustain a witness to the unsaid. We find ourselves always at the threshold of a philosophical problem. The loss of the apodicticity of consciousness in the search for the subject as a result of psychoanalytic theory turns the light-metaphor of rationalistic epistemologies over to a technique of the night that recognizes in dreams a work revealing an imaginal ego or metaphorical subject. An unspoken ontology belongs to this subjectivity that cannot be found in what Freud says but does stand as a correlative achievement of the unsaid.

Freudian thought is not just another example of our problem. Psychoanalytic antiphenomenology and philosophical phenomenology collide just at that point where an archaeology of the imagination becomes an epistemology of darkness. The conscious image is a representation and not a presentation. It is a presence that reveals an absence. Its presence in a semantics of meaning is only a trace of the force that is absent. If we insist on a translation of an economics of force into a semantics of meaning, we realize that we have shifted to discourse of a second order that can only speak of darkness in the first order. This second order is discourse about discourse. Of course, it too is subject to the force of its own critique and ceases to light the way once we acknowledge the possibility for a reflexive regression. We continually return to a disjunction between realms of force and meaning even if the semantics of meaning has as its object an articulation of realms of force.

It is apparent to the sensitive reader of Freud that Freudian discourse attempts to be a mixed discourse intermingling questions of meaning and force.[10] Force language (cathexis, anticathexis, repression, etc.), determinations of meaning (dreams, symptoms, culture), and mythological language (Eros, Thanatos, and Ananke) intersect in a topographical map of the psyche. This map is not the exclusive property of psychoanalysis, nor is it a problem only for psychoanalysis. The force/meaning disjunction is an idiomatic expression of the mind/body disjunction that is a general problem for all reflective inquiry. What we have discovered is an impassable passage.

This aporia in the middle of both philosophical and psychoanalytic reflection can be defined clearly when we hold fast to what is given in our experience of language through language. Phenomenological bracketing of the linguistic world sets up the problem. When we are not able to appeal beyond language in an understanding of language, we immediately notice that the elemental units of language stand by themselves naked and empty. The signifier does not contain the signified. In itself it is empty and stands only as an inscription, a marking, or an image. The phenomenology of language describes a dialectic of presence and absence that acknowledges the mystery of a world made present through the emptiness of signs.[11] If we maintain the phenomenological reduction, fix our gaze on the semantics of meaning, we understand that the presence we experience is the dialectical otherness residing in the unsaid, the order of the unrealized or unconscious.

The problem is experienced more radically in writing than in speaking. What is romantically thought to be the unity of thought-sound disappears in the written text, and there we come face to face with the emptiness of the signifier. Derrida's emphasis on the priority of writing over speech leads us toward a strong statement of the disjunction between force and meaning. The distrust and fear of the violence of writing in Saussure and Rousseau is a resistance to the wound suffered by consciousness when we realize that the semantics of meaning within the control of conscious reflection is always empty when examined as it presents itself.[12] In writing, the signifier can be separated from the signified, and therein lies its danger for a romantic conception of the phonological unity of consciousness that claims to receive rather than intend or construct a world. The phonic substance is neutralized by writing, and the signifier is left, without benefit of gesture or proximity, to be anything other than what it is.[13]

In fact, Derrida inverts the dependency relationship between speech and writing in his notion of arche-writing so that writing has ontological priority over speech. "Arche-writing, at first the possibility of the spoken word, then of the '*graphie*' in the narrow sense, the birthplace of 'usurpation,' denounced from Plato to Saussure, this trace is the opening of the first exteriority in general, the enigmatic relationship of the living to its other and of an inside to an outside: spacing."[14]

This is not a denial of a realm of force or Being behind the manifest content of language expressions. It is an acknowledgment that the unsaid and its idiomatic corollaries are present only as a trace that is itself effaced by the nature of language usage. The presence of an absence, a gap, is what gives meaning to the realm of force that constitutes the first meaning of the unconscious. It is not the denial but the repression of such forces that constitutes our problem and defines the aporia. The linguistic achievement is a very strange kind of repression. Derrida's use of the word "effacement" is an apt description of the creation of an absence through a presence. Effacement of the forces that press upon or against consciousness is not a simple negation. A transformation from one realm of connectedness to another actually occurs. We might want to borrow a Hegelian notion and call this process "sublation." The economic relationships among forces are effaced, repressed, since the image of the force has ceased to be a force and is instead now a signifier dependent on rules of syntax and limited in use by the determinations of a lexicographer.

The linguistic achievement is a creating of consciousness. A theory of language and a theory of consciousness are so intertwined that the delineation of one theory becomes an interpretation of the other. We should expect that a philosophy of consciousness entails a parallel philosophy of language and that a philosophy of language entails a parallel philosophy of consciousness. For example, Bloom's "map of misprision" directly correlated rhetorical tropes with psychoanalytically determined psychic defenses.[15] A complex theory of language requires a complex theory of consciousness and, inversely, a complex theory of consciousness requires a complex theory of language. Even to develop a concept as complex as the unconscious, we need a language that can be creatively troped so it reveals that its presence is an absence. This speaking of the unsaid is a gain in meaning that is the primary signification for the abstract concept of the unconscious.

Freud's claim that we can only know the unconscious as something conscious—"after it has undergone transformation or translation into something conscious"—is the metapsychological expression of what we are calling the central epistemological problem.[16] The translation into something conscious is the translation into a mental image. Since the image is not identical with a force or external reality (it marks its absence), we must understand the image as the result of work. It is not sufficient to say that image-making is the work of the imagination, because image-making is how we define the imagination. We are still left with the question of determining the conditions of imaginal thinking. The concept of the imagination is a metaphor to give an account of image-making. It is a possibility for consciousness and also a convoluted expression of consciousness.

The nature of the connection between force and meaning, instinct and image, can only be explored within a semantics of meaning, because the forces remain unsaid except as they are disclosed *as the absence in the presence of the signifier*. Neither psychoanalysis nor phenomenology ever confront bare forces.[17] The closest we come to force is in the experience of the link between instinct and image. When language usage is highly sedimented it is possible to forget that the achievement of consciousness depends on a mixed discourse overdetermined in realms of force and meaning, because it is possible to become fascinated with the exteriority of semantic connections. The crossword puzzle of signifiers can posit itself as a supplementary signification that obscures the significance of the intersection of meaning and force. The interrelation of signifiers is a presence that often becomes so bright or noisy that the absence ceases to be noticed.

We must deliberately choose to go into the night of our experience to be hearers of the unsaid word. We must take the residue of the daylight world into the night if we are to work in the authentic ambiguity of mixed discourse. Although we can only begin with what is present, we can use present signifiers to locate the spaces and silences. We use language to disrupt its own sedimentation. The image of interpretation as a deconstruction becomes clearer. "To interpret is to displace the origin of meaning to another region."[18] In psychoanalytic theory, the displacement takes us to the heart of mixed discourse where desire is represented through image. Displacement should not be confused with substitution. Interpretation that acknowledges mixed discourse cannot be satisfied with analogical substitutions that are really only elaborations of what is present by extension of connections between signifiers. Analogy thus defers an encounter with the primal language of origination.

The displacement that occurs in psychoanalytic interpretation alters our thinking about thinking. As Jacques Lacan has pointed out, "analogy is not metaphor," and it was through avoiding analogy that Freud opened up the interpretation of dreams.[19] He avoided analogy because it forgot the energies of the psyche. The relationship to language that we discover in psychoanalytic interpretation negates a semantics of meaning controlled by consciousness. The commitment to mixed discourse that emerges is characterized by Ricoeur as a semantics of desire.[20] A semantics of desire falls, like all discourse, within a semantics of meaning. It is a special discourse in that it allows space for influence of the unconscious or unconscious motivation. This is explicit in the content of Freud's case studies but I want to suggest that a mixed discourse is achieved not in content but in space provided for the unsaid. There is room in Freud's thought for the liberation of image in the dark night of reality.

Freud's sensitivity to the magic of language and the announcement of meanings in what usually passes as trivial gives us a clue about the passage into a mixed discourse.

> Words were originally magic and to this day words have retained much
> of their ancient magical power. . . . Thus we shall not depreciate the use
> of words in psychotherapy and we shall be pleased if we can listen to
> the words that pass between the analyst and his patient.[21]

The magic requires a listening to what is unsaid in those words that pass between the analyst and patient. If we pay attention to what Freud does in his "saying," we again note a parallel concern with Heidegger's expression of the need to seek out a neighborhood where thinking and poetry dwell.[22] "Let us stay with the most urgent issue, which is, to seek out the neighborhood of poetry and thinking— which now means the encounter of the two facing each other."[23] This is where we can listen to the grant of language by allowing for the voice of mixed discourse.

The ontic-ontological disjunction and the meaning-force disjunction are not equatable within a semantics of meaning. They do, however, bear witness to the mysterious promise of language and displace the grant of language from the realm of conscious control. Freud's long route through the phenomenality of psychological experience and metapsychological theory obscures the significance of the consulting room as a neighborhood for poetic indwelling. His own insistence on the scientific character of his work obscures Freud the literary figure, a thinker who struggled with the mythological forces of Eros, Thanatos, and Ananke in a primal scene of poetic achievement. It is the achievement of Freud's doing by his saying and not the content of his theories that even allows for the comparison I am making with Heidegger. It is also here that Freud becomes an important figure for developing a genre of discourse consonant with an epistemology of darkness.

The rereading of Freud I am suggesting is not a negative evaluation of the content of his metapsychological theories; that judgment is bracketed. Independent of the judgment concerning the adequacy of the content of those theories, the formulation of his theories carried ordinary experience into the spaces of metaphorical and poetic thinking. Independent of Freud's conscious intention, although not necessarily contrary to it, his work is paradigmatic of a *telling* that is a *showing* and blazes a path of metaphorical thinking.

Several movements and recognitions in the development of case histories make room for the imaginative achievement of poetic sensibilities. First, the one rule of psychoanalytic treatment is a release of language that is an affront to conscious control. "The next day I made him pledge himself to submit to the one and only condition of treatment—namely to say everything that came into his head, even if it was unpleasant to him, or seemed unimportant, or irrelevant or senseless."[24] Language was no longer immediately subject to its sedimentation as determined by conscious judgment. His metapsychology suggested that there would be gaps in a supposed stream of consciousness and even in the knowledge of what we are saying. He even noted that "the patients themselves do not know the wording of their own obsessional ideas."[25] Both the first requisite of treatment and the metapsychological theory of gaps, ellipses, and not knowing make space for the unsaid voice of mixed discourse.

Second, in the development of a case history, Freud intrudes on narrative with the introduction of dissimilar constructions that trope the narrative as a linguistic genre in a way that resembles the troping by a metaphorical construction in a sentence. Although we usually think of metaphor as something that happens to a noun, the concept of metaphor is much larger than this designation even in the classic rhetoric of Aristotle.[26] Aristotle also defines metaphor in terms of a displacement or movement (epiphora). ". . . One could say that epiphora is a process that concerns the semantic kernel, not just of the noun and verb but of all meaningful linguistic entities, and that this process designates change of meaning as such."[27] If we work with an enlarged concept of metaphor that includes whole units of discourse, we recognize in Freud's case histories a displacement that is a movement and change of meaning as such. Analysis becomes a vessel of metaphorical interchange. Freud's histories are a model of working in the rhetoric of poesis. It is not a noun but narrative discourse itself that is troped.

It is easy to miss this movement in Freud if our investigation is limited to the sentence as the only semantic unit that can house displacement and alter meaning. The plot of psychoanalytic retellings always involves the mystery of repression surrounding what appears to be a primal scene of desire enacted, fantasized, threatened, or threatening. What appear to be trivial memories are shifted into a powerful drama of psychosexual complexities that are themselves the traces of a primal scene of violence and sexuality.

In collaboration with a patient Freud displaced the symptoms and symbols of the wholly personal story through the interjection of a primal scene that was overdetermined in what might be called mythological history and the mythopoeic forces of Eros, Thanatos, and Ananke. The eye for seeing the personal story in the dissimilar realm of the mythopoeic is one of Freud's great achievements. Certainly we cannot expect a primal scene with mythological components to be a simple memory of the patient.

> All that I mean to say is this: scenes, like this one in my present patient's case, which date from such an early period and exhibit a similar content, and which further lay claim to such an extraordinary significance for the history of the case, are as a rule not reproduced as recollections, but have to be divined—constructed—gradually and laboriously from an aggregate of indications.[28]

Freud then goes on to suggest that he would be glad to know if the primal scene is a fantasy or real experience, but admits that this is not a question of real importance.[29]

Of real importance, however, is that through the troping of the personal narrative the patient experiences a new consciousness— new memories.[30] This is the only test of the adequacy of constructions introduced into the case history. What this means becomes clearer when Freud compares construction in analysis with reconstruction in archaeology. The difference he notes is that for the archaeologist the reconstruction is the goal while for the analyst it is a preliminary endeavor. "The analyst finishes a piece of construction and communicates it to the subject of the analysis so that it may work upon him."[31] The constructions effect a movement (epiphora) and can be viewed as metaphorizing personal narrative. The storytelling of case histories is brought into the neighborhood where thinking and poetry face each other. The introduction of a primal language against the horizon of a primal scene is a metaphorical intrusion that "works" on the patient in the emergence of a new consciousness. Freud's achievement is a raid on the prosaic world of dreary normality: it makes space for mixed discourse that draws us nearer to the excitement of the realm of force.

Freud has, through the troping of ordinary language usage, "restored to psychotherapy the realm of inner space."[32] We are able to come closer to that dark inaccessible part of our personality, "a cauldron full of seething excitations,"[33] as an achievement of mixed discourse. In fact, both the claim and achievement of Freud place in front of us a paradigm for the intersection of dissimilar realms of connection, a paradigm that expresses a limited solution to the problem of an epistemology of darkness. Freud links two realms in the practice of psychoanalysis without dissolving one into the other. Here we see the metapsychology as a heuristic method and not as an explanation of the semantics of desire. Troping the narrative is a solvent that creates a specific solution. Freud provides an important specific example but not a general answer to the problem we have defined.

The general importance of psychoanalytic reflection for us is that it points to an ontology of understanding.[34] Language (in Freud the mixed discourse of meaning and desire) is implicated in forces that give a significance to the work of language so that that work is self-transcendent. Language speaks reality even if we don't want it to speak at all. Representation creates spaces and silences that hold us close to reality. The emptying of linguistic reality into what appears to be a deconstructive nihilism can paradoxically constitute consent to the significance of extralinguistic reality marked only by the presence that is an absence. It is important to note that the deployment of meaning that is referred to as the extralinguistic significance of language takes place in those spaces and silences that are characteristically dark in a semantics of meaning.

Mixed discourse is an invitation into the darkness that is at the same time a call for the liberation of the image from the narrow confines of literal signification. Spaces and silences are conditions for the possibility of open-ended discourse that is also a mixed discourse. The spaces and silences haunt the codification of intertextual relations in a linguistic system and functionally overdetermine the system in the realm of absences by their presence. With or without a theory of symbolic relations to extralinguistic realities, language is itself already a lived experience that transcends its abstract intelligibility. Language usage cannot escape the promise and burden of being a mixed discourse (even in moments of denial of this characteristic). The representation of denial is based on a first-order repression that is a primary act of what is supposedly denied. We are back to that oxymoronic state of affairs where antithetical meanings are primary meanings. We consent to the knowing that is not-knowing and the said that is unsaid. This consent is a refusal and an ecstasy. We refuse language usage its self-containment and experience the ecstasy of the self-transcendence of language in extralinguistic realms.

The archaeological investigation of the imagination returns to its beginning: it has uncovered the image. The sought-for first principles are not metaphysical artifacts but are instead heuristic principles for what can become diverse methods of hesitation before the fullness of images. This claim is neither passive nor skeptical. There is work to do. Consent to the darkness of spaces and silences needs to be thematized and articulated. This is the work of foundational theology, and it is a hermeneutics of the imagination. Here, "interpretation is at the hinge between linguistics and nonlinguistics, between language and lived experience."[35] Interpretation, as in Freud, situates itself as a mixed discourse.

A place remains for historical and descriptive studies that work within a semantics of meaning in the collecting of images and in the conservation of our linguistic and experiential inheritance. The importance of exact scholarship in determining a population of concepts complements constructive thinking, but neither is a substitute for the other. The constructive work of theology and other disciplines of the imagination follows from the acknowledgment that there is a word hidden in the word. The irony is that construction looks like deconstruction. Constructive thinking tropes both literary and experiential texts to provide both spaces and silences for the liberation of the image. It is a creative work and a movement. We can characterize the future of imaginal thinking as linguistic violence but we cannot chart its path, because it will be a journey into the darkness of the spaces and silences. Each discipline of the imagination will have to create a genre of mixed discourse appropriate to its task, and each discipline will have to critique itself from inside its discursive achievement to chart the possibilities that reside in the dark spaces of its achievement.

NOTES

1. Edmund Jabès, *The Book of Questions* (Middletown, Conn.: Wesleyan University Press, 1972), 90.

2. Michel Foucault, *Madness and Civilization: A History of Insanity in the Age of Reason* (New York: Vintage Books, 1973), 103–4.

3. Ibid., 94.

4. Martin Heidegger, *On Time and Being* (New York: Harper & Row, 1972), 2.

5. Harold Bloom, *A Map of Misreading* (New York: Oxford Univ. Press, 1975), 41–62; Jacques Derrida, *Writing and Difference* (Chicago: Univ. of Chicago Press, 1978), 196–231.

6. Thomas J. J. Altizer, *The Self-Embodiment of God* (New York: Harper & Row, 1977), 10.

7. Martin Heidegger, *Being and Time* (New York: Harper & Row, 1962), 59.

8. Martin Heidegger, *On the Way to Language* (New York: Harper & Row, 1971), 81.

9. Martin Heidegger, *Existence and Being* (Chicago: Regnery Gateway Edition), 283.

10. Paul Ricoeur, *The Conflict of Interpretations* (Evanston, Ill.: Northwestern Univ. Press, 1974), 160.

11. Cf. Paul Ricoeur, *Freud and Philosophy: An Essay on Interpretation* (New Haven, Conn.: Yale Univ. Press, 1970), 384–85.

12. Jacques Derrida, *Of Grammatology* (Baltimore: Johns Hopkins Univ. Press, 1974).

13. Ibid., 62.

14. Ibid., 70.

15. Bloom, *Map of Misreading*, 84.

16. Sigmund Freud, *The Standard Edition of the Complete Psychological Works of Sigmund Freud*, 24 vols. (London: Hogarth Press and the Institute of Psychoanalysis, 1953–74), 14:166.

17. Ricoeur, *Freud and Philosophy*, 151.

18. Ibid., 91.

19. Jacques Lacan, *Écrits: A Selection* (New York: W. W. Norton, 1977), 53.

20. Ricoeur, *Freud and Philosophy*, 363.

21. Freud, *Complete Psychological Works*, 15:17.

22. Heidegger, *On the Way to Language*, 80.

23. Ibid., 82.

24. Freud, *Complete Psychological Works*, 10:159.

25. Ibid., 223.

26. Paul Ricoeur, *The Rule of Metaphor: Multi-disciplinary Studies of the Creation of Meaning in Language* (Toronto: Univ. of Toronto Press, 1977), 16–17.

27. Ibid., 17.

28. Freud, *Complete Psychological Works*, 17:51.

29. Ibid., 97.
30. Ibid., 23:262.
31. Ibid., 260.
32. James Hillman, *The Dream and the Underworld* (New York: Harper & Row, 1979), 16.
33. Freud, *Complete Psychological Works*, 12:73.
34. Ricoeur, *Conflict of Interpretation*, 20.
35. Ibid., 66.

4

Metaphor and the Accession to Theological Language

Mark the first page of the book with a red marker. For, in the beginning, the wound is invisible. —Reb Alce[1]

— Edmund Jabès

Theology is writing. Sometimes it is implicit writing, but it is always within the referential order of language. Religion is not always writing. The philosophy of religion is writing. Sometimes it is implicit writing, but it is always within the referential order of language.

Theology and the philosophy of religion are related to religion, and they are related to each other. It is easy to ascertain that their relationship to each other is semantic, but their relationship to religion is enigmatic. Theology sometimes sees itself as religion and the philosophy of religion sometimes sees its relationship to theology as a relationship to religion. Theology seldom sees itself as religion without a remainder, and the philosophy of religion usually recognizes this nonidentity. Whether the choice is to serve religion or to analyze it, one should acknowledge that neither philosophy nor theology can contain religion or fully substitute themselves for it. The enigmatic relationship of writing disciplines to religion is a reflection on writing and a reflection of religion.

Writing is repression. Theology is writing. Theology is repression. The philosophy of religion is writing. The philosophy of religion is repression. The writing disciplines contiguous to religion are in their origin a repression of religion, except in those instances when religion is itself writing.

The claim that accession to theological language is repression hinges on the two claims that writing is repression and that theology is writing. Neither claim is a direct result of theological thinking. Both result from thinking about thinking and presuppose meaning as representational. It is when writing becomes conscious of itself as representational that it knows itself as repression rather than as revelation.

The choice to focus on theological writing instead of theological speaking is an attempt to gain clarity in understanding the accession to theological language. When a text is spoken it is often difficult to hear the text itself and not confuse it with the voice of the text. But that same text is capable of being written, and it is not incidental that language is capable of being written.[2] In writing, the production of a text is disjoined from the fullness of speech-events because a text can stand by itself once written. It becomes a thing beside other things and is freed from the circumstance of origination. It no longer belongs to its author and the privacy of the author's intention. It resides among other texts in the order of language.

I do not mean to suggest that the organic complexity of speech or the author's intention are unimportant and do not present herme- neutical problems. However, the examination of the abstract ideality of the text most easily isolated in writing gives us insight into language functioning that can be obscured without this isolation.

First, the fact that the text can stand alone gives us a clue to the meaning of writing. Writing lifts experience into the order of language. Experience is transformed so that through a dialectic of presence and absence it is no longer identical with itself. Object language, written or spoken, evokes an object through a substitute that is not the object. "The word is the presence of the thing it designates and posits it 'in itself' in its order of reality. Two separate but referential orders are thus ordered by the act of designation; the *real* and *language*."[3] In the realm of language, the written text stands on a new stage and can be separated from author and original context. This is still possible even if we argue that the separation is a violation of the author's intention. This possibility is realized by the fact of the written text. The text has its own ontological status and can be evaluated as it presents itself.

Second, a written text presents itself in its own materiality. Phonetic elements are complemented by and sometimes displaced by picto- graphic and ideogrammatic elements not translatable into speech. This is particularly evident in hieroglyphic writings. The materiality of the written text can be likened to the steel or stone of the sculptor and the oils or acrylics of the painter, although a difference must also be acknowledged. The likeness resides in the density of an ontological trace, and the difference is in the ontic display of media dissimilarities. Ironically, the acknowledgment of a likeness is determined amidst the material similarity of alternative media. The act of deferring, differing, and repeating creates and fills a space that is at once a presence and a representation. The presence is a representation of what is absent because of the deferring that is necessarily a differing. What is deferred is no longer present so that what is present differs from what is deferred.[4]

Once a distinction is made between the order of the real and the order of language, most of us would like to cast our lot with the order of the real if we only could escape the bell jar that would descend upon this decision and silence its presence. The order of the real cannot even house cries or screams that are primitive representational presences once the real has been distinguished from the order of language. Language is a phenomenon in the order of the real only through the substance and texture of its own textuality. In the order of the real a cry is only a cry. It has meaning only in the order of language. When we appeal to referential determinations within this textual fabric, we have entered the order of language.

We can speak or we can be silent. If we speak, our speech can be transformed into writing, and it then becomes difficult to deny that we have chosen to live within the order of language. Of course this is not an escape from the order of the real. First-order experience belongs to the order of the real and the law of this house—the economics of force. The experience of experience belongs to the linguistic order, and within this house we can talk about a semantics of meaning. This distinction is complicated by the recognition that although the experience *of* experience is described as being of a second order and within a semantics of meaning, as experience it is of the first order and also belongs to an economics of force. The semantics of meaning is itself overdetermined in an economics of force. There is an inside and outside to second-order experience, and it is the inside that we are calling a semantics of meaning. Although the outside resides in what we mean from the inside by reality, whatever we know of the outside is known through the deployment of images on the inside. The epistemological dilemma is that what has an inside presence is an absence of the outside.

The populations of signs, words, and concepts within a semantics of meaning are present only to each other. The references are textual or intertextual. The text can be layered, but there is still no text but the present text.[5] A consent to the givenness of experience insists on bracketing texts and seeing them in their own materiality. We surrender a natural attitude that naively identifies first- and second-order experience. We might want to say that the materiality of language intrudes on the fantasy that direct experience is available to intelligence without being transformed by thinking. The economics of force is itself a concept within a semantics of meaning. This disjunction at the heart of our work again appears to be an aporia, an impassable passage, that confronts us with the danger of a skeptical immobilization.

Theology accompanied by other writing disciplines often hesitates when this originating wound of thinking becomes visible. When the passage to primary experience is blocked by the nature of its own linguistic achievement, theology finds itself restricted to the space of this achievement. A semantic anxiety develops that has been described by Harold Bloom as an anxiety of influence.[6] What he calls "the melancholy of the creative mind's desperate insistence upon priority"[7] and the need to "clear imaginative space"[8] for writing combine to form the problem not only of modern poetry but also of theology. In the restricted space of linguistic presence we soon discover that behind and beyond theology is only more theology. Our space is crowded by precursors and contemporaries, and unless theology can get to a source that is more primal than itself, new theology appears only to be a repetition or pedagogical tool.

The recent offspring of theological hesitations are expressions of methodological narcissism and obscurantist spiritualities. Both are disguises for theological thinking, although in a more restricted space than that of the first hesitation. Positivistic withdrawals and declarations of the end of theology are repressions of tradition that first appear to clear a limited space. The clearing is illusory. By saying what theology cannot say, negative theologies live within the materiality of the tradition. The training for negative theology is positive theology, since it shares in the materiality of the tradition. That is, declaring the end of theology is possible only because of the persistence of theology. It can even be said that the act of limiting theology is a theological writing contributing to the persistence of theology. The important contribution of negative theologies is that they demonstrate the vitality of theological thinking without the constraints of literalism but within the constraints of language. Negative theologies live with semantic anxiety and conserve the resources of the linguistic tradition even if they are unhappy within this constriction.

On the other hand, the appeal to primary experience in new spiritualities is usually little more than an abandonment of a rich linguistic tradition for an impoverished use of language in which the touch, sigh, or cry are substituted for more complex semantic constructions and bodily amplifications of feelings are substituted for more complex secondary experiences. The problem has not been solved. This denial of complexity is still within a semantics of meaning and is dependent on image formation for its deployment. The appeal to feeling is representational, and the references are to each other. There is still a presence that marks an absence. The impoverishment of the language of presence simply means that the experience of experience is a text with little texture.

A more familiar and traditional response to radical disjunctions between reality and meaning is the search for a new foundation or a return to originating experience. The discovery of a primal ground coincides with an effacement of history, an erasure of linguistic achievement leaving a *tabula rasa* ready for reconstruction through fresh markings. In both examples the resolution of the aporia is thought to be possible through rigorous work. It is thought that the aporia has manifested itself because the thinking that crowds our space was inadequate or misguided. The underlying assumption is that we have encountered an aporia because we ventured down the wrong road. It is suggested that we need a new starting point and a new road. In its most naive expression, this quest begins with an assessment of semantic anxiety as an inappropriate response to what may be thought of as no more important than a category mistake. In its more critical expressions, some sophisticated isomorphism between reality and language is transformed into a hypostasis of language. The trace of force is erased and we are left with a linguistic realism, sometimes a literalism. Ironically, the enfranchisement of language with weight of a descriptive realism is a forgetfulness of language. What is absent is thought to be present and what is present is ignored.

When language convolutes and shows itself rather than feigning transparency to an objective world, we sometimes see this as a failure of language. What we are experiencing is that language, once written, can stand independently of our individual consciousness. What is first thought to be a failure is better described as a wound, and what is wounded is the claim that language follows consciousness and remains in its control. The subversion of consciousness through distortion of language in the psychopathology of everyday life and the transcendence of consciousness in the revelatory power of language are exemplary displays of the dislocation of the subject from the controlling center of linguistic experience. The subject discovers itself as one object beside others in the linguistic achievement that marks the presence of the subject. This presence also reveals an absence. The epistemological dilemma dresses itself in psychological meaning but is still a philosophical problem.

Foucault describes the problem as a loss of philosophical subjectivity. "The breakdown of philosophical subjectivity and its dispersion in a language that dispossesses it while multiplying it in the space created by its absence is probably one of the fundamental structures of contemporary thought."[9] The convolution of language, misshapen and craglike, "refers to itself and is folded back on a questioning of its limits."[10] What language discovers is more language. It is this enclosure of language in a nondialectic semantic display that frustrates the return to origins or the search for foundation. Within the semantic order one metaphor is only substituted for another. The dialectic between force and meaning is conspicuous by its absence.

Ironically, subjectivity is lost in all attempts to fix its origin or foundation. It is given over to the referential interiority of the text. Subjectivity is not extinguished. It is simply displaced into the order of its own creation. Language becomes "the being-there of the mind," and "this 'reality of language' is nothing other than the meaning achieved by a behavior."[11] Total reflection is impossible. Language can only mirror consciousness within the limited dimensionality of language. Total reflection is a concept that would dissolve the dialectical tension between force and meaning that is the first moment of its possibility. Theology is not going to found itself in radical reflection. It is going to have to live in the tension of a crowded marketplace of ideas and language.

The great temptation of a postcritical theology is silence. The silence that can follow a critical hesitation is not a retreat, but a goal that must be achieved. This would not be a simple achievement: we are already in language. In the recent work of Thomas Altizer we see just how complex it is to talk about a theological silence, and paradoxically we find ourselves still speaking. He notes that silence is both the origin and the end of speech.[12] It is the limit we have encountered as a frustration to the quest for origins or foundations.

The journey to the beginning and the journey to the end are indiscernible. We come to silence.

Altizer's active meditation on silence issues in an apocalyptic metaphor of total presence. This speaking of a total presence is a proleptic image that contrasts with the eschatological realization it anticipates. The eschatological reality is silent, and yet we keep on speaking. "Once speech has spoken, its voice establishes a world or a field, and that field is indissoluble, it cannot simply disappear or pass away."[13] He affirms that speech ends only at the dawning of a totally present actuality. The word could no longer be written. This return to an origin that is also an end is not a return to the book but to the body.

Altizer continues to write. In the continuation of writing lies a clue to the meaning of theology. The metaphor of total presence is a negation. "Final presence can only have a negative identity to any integral or individual form of consciousness, therefore it will be wholly manifest to that consciousness as judgment, and as total judgment which consumes all given and individual identity."[14]

Theology has been a transgressor. It has been both prophetic and parabolic in its negation of a sedimented linguistic world, to the point that it is willing to entertain language in an extreme distention of intelligibility bordering on silence. If we catalogue the tradition we continually stumble over images of the apocalypse, intimations of that than which nothing greater can be conceived, characteristic forms of angelic knowledge, rumors of ineffable meanings, and other troped constructions within a semantics of meaning that wrestle with ordinary uses of language. When we have wrestled with whatever are our demons and are blessed with a new name, that name can be written and theology continues.

Theology does not cease to be transgressive. It is a work and not a solution. The deployment of eschatological formulas such as Thomas Altizer's total presence or Anselm's supreme conceptuality are deconstructions of sedimented worlds of language. Theology, in all its creative moments, is deconstructive of a crowded linguistic space, and it is here that we see its future. It is our experience of language that describes a purpose for this activity. In particular, the accession to theological language is an explicit valuation of language turned against the achievement of a visible world of textual meanings. This turning against is also a receiving of the text. Tropes, transgressions, misreadings, misprision are all references to the word-event that describes the work of a deconstructivist hermeneutic. We engage ourselves with the theological tradition to make space for more theological thinking. It is the work and not its content that is the first-order theological achievement. It is the work that lives in the dialectic between force and meaning.

Speech and writing create a virtual space that is the possibility for a work of language. It is a space for unlimited reduplication and repetition. There are no limits on how many times language can fold on itself. In this sense its internal manifestation is unconditional. Foucault says that it is in this "virtual space where speech discovers the endless resourcefulness of its own image and where it can represent itself as already existing behind itself, already active beyond itself, to infinity."[15] One must carefully note that this fecundity is representational and lies in the semantic realm. This disclaimer, however, is an expression of the meaning of language acts and not a diminishment of their meaning. The celebration of poetic freedom is an acute consciousness of language itself. Language can reference itself in an unlimited display of possibilities. We accordingly come to enjoy meaning but cannot ascertain that these fictions are in concord with the economy of forces that press round about this moment of freedom.

The reflection that enables us to elaborate the disjunction between meaning and force is an achievement within the realm of meaning that exemplifies language turning on itself. Language determines within itself an indeterminate relationship to reality that is at the same time an expression of its reality. Language transcends the forces to which it indeterminately refers, but it cannot transcend itself. It can only subvert itself so that its transcendence of primary forces is compromised. The indeterminacy of this breach is experienced as a loss of meaning within the semantic realm. Words and images are quickly deployed to cover the gap, and the breach is then experienced as meaningful. It is of course no longer itself but a re-presentation. All that has been ascertained is that language and the semantics of meaning do not include reality but dwell in the neighborhood of nonlinguistic forces. This, however, is an important recognition from within language. It may be as close a rapprochement between the disjunctive realms of force and meaning as can be achieved within the realm of language. We cannot turn to the realm of force, because its sense is mute until represented in language. The breaching of the disjunction only has meaning when it is reduplicated in the realm of language, which is at the same time the reaffirmation of the disjunction. Whatever we mean by reality is always appearing and appearance.

Appearance or coming to appear is not sham or falsity. It is how experience comes to stand in speech and writing. The concept of appearance can also be an internal signifier of the closure of language as a system. As such it is an enigmatic concept, because it has an indeterminate reference outside itself. *Appearance* is at the same time an overdetermined and an indeterminate concept. It is overdetermined since it is connected not only to a semantics of meaning but also to the economics of force. It is indeterminate since the connection to the realm of force is a breach that becomes meaningful only when represented in the semantics of meaning.

Jacques Derrida speaks to this problem when he says,

> Since language has not fallen from the sky, it is clear that the differences have been produced; they are effects produced, but effects that do not have as their cause a subject or substance, a thing in general, or a being that is somewhere present and itself escapes the play of difference.[16]

He has defined the problem so that a closed system of language is experienced as incomplete. He then acknowledges that

> I have tried to indicate a way out of the closure imposed by this system, namely, by means of the "trace." No more an effect than a cause, the "trace" cannot of itself, taken outside of its context, suffice to bring about the required transgression.[17]

The path that he has indicated is still the path of language. The only possibility he has shown as a way out of language is to follow the way of language.

The trace marks the breach and as such is also a hinge. The trace would have no meaning without the breach, but the meaning of the breach is determined only as it is deferred toward semantic representation. The appearance of the trace, that which gives it its difference in the semantic realm, is a sign of unresolved overdetermination. It is a lucid metaphor, a metaphor of metaphoricity. A lucid metaphor appears in terms of its metaphoricity. The hinge between the disjunctive realms of force and meaning must be metaphorical, because the hinge has meaning as part of a semantic display. It is a metaphorical display of a metaphorical act. A similarity is discerned between dissimilar domains. The troping of a word within a text is layered over the breaching of the limits of textuality and appears in what is textually present as a coincidence of meaning. The similarity between what is dissimilar is only an apparent similarity; but this is no surprise since the meaning of a text is in its appearance. The "trace" appears and then disappears in a *mimesis* of its own metaphorical character.

Its indeterminate meaning is substituted for its determinate meaning
in a system of textual references, and this is why it appears only to
disappear.

The trace marks a fissure within language. It stops textual intrasig-
nification from coming to complete expression. It is a momentary
clearing within the work of language where we can pose the question
of what lies beyond language. We are able to ask, What have we
forgotten? The trajectory of this question can be expressed but not
contained within a semantics of meaning. The trace enfranchises the
question of an extralinguistic reality, and the scale of our inquiry has
been altered. We need a different frame for attending to the importance
of questions that violate the semantic framework in which they are
enclosed. We need a place for language to "say" and "show" more
than its internal content.

Paul Ricoeur suggests that to move to another framework is to shift
from semantics to hermeneutics. He affirms that in a general theory
of symbolism overdetermination refers to semantic and nonsemantic
patterns of relationship. His concept of hermeneutics depends on the
fundamental condition

> that symbolics is the means of expressing an extralinguistic reality. This
> is of the greatest importance for the subsequent confrontation; antici-
> pating an expression which will take on its precise meaning only on
> another strategic level, I will say that in hermeneutics there is no closed
> system of the universe of signs.[18]

Although I agree with Ricoeur that there is no closed system of the
universe of signs, we should not confuse this claim with the hope for
a symbolic realism that searches the contours of a semantics of
meaning for nonsemantic realities. The dilemma of semantic captivity
is not that easily resolved. Within the realm of semantic meaning, all
that we will see is the text that presents itself. In the text the forces
are present only as an absence. The symbol can reside in a semantic
text only as a metaphor, and we can talk about an extralinguistic
reference only if it is a lucid metaphor. Even then it is language
referencing its own nature.

The notion of the symbol is developed within language and marks
a point around which language can turn or fold on itself. It is in this
second order of reflexivity that the symbol is mirrored as a lucid
metaphor. The need for a hermeneutical framework is secondarily
derived from the symbol but primarily derived from the lucid
metaphor. This is just one of the peculiar qualities of language when

it folds on and mirrors itself. We are still within language, and I have focused on the shift from symbol to metaphor to emphasize that hermeneutics is implied by the metaphoricity of language.

Language—the presence of an absence—is metaphorical by its very deployment. It substitutes meaning for force. Marking the similarity of the dissimilar realms of force and meaning can only be an achievement of metaphor. The force disappears paradoxically in the substitution that constitutes its appearance in a realm of meaning. This means that the lucidity of the metaphor is reflexive. It reveals its own nature but not the nature of the forces that have disappeared. Force is repressed as force to be revealed as meaning.

Hermeneutics is a work and movement in language that turns language on itself. We can best understand its importance if we contrast its movement with the first order of a semantic achievement. The semantic achievement of language is to bring force to meaning. This work is a transformation and a repression. Meaning is substituted for force and what we hold in consciousness is meaning. In contrast, hermeneutics as we have conceived it brings meaning to force. This is a movement and not a transformation. It remains within the semantic realm. Force is not substituted for meaning. What we hold in consciousness is meaning. However, our hold has become tenuous. The meaning that we hold on to is metaphorical. The meaning of meaning, language folded on itself, brings us to the recognition of the absence that is present as the achievement of language. Meaning is brought to force, gives recognition to force, but does not become force. We come to dwell at the foundation of conscious meaning without surrendering consciousness. The lucid metaphor in its inde-terminacy is especially permeable to the forces of origination that language brings to meaning. The critical violence of hermeneutical inquiry releases consciousness from its sedimentation by self-inflicted wounds that are at the same time openings for the transformation of force into meaning. We are allowed a second naivete. Forces are freshly reduplicated in a metaphorical deployment. A postcritical text is formed.

We begin to understand why theology fashioned as a hermeneutical movement must be transgressive. The hermeneutical task is not the exegesis of a precritical or postcritical text. Exegesis is another task that has been traditionally assumed by theology in the dissemination and sedimentation of meaning. It has a linear function in the extension of meaning that is also a further sedimentation. The hermeneutical exigency appears when language is forced back on itself in the crowded marketplace of ideas. When the reflexive wound appears hermeneutical thinking takes on a special urgency, because we are acutely conscious that exegesis is a textual repetition that solidifies the repression of primal forces. Force is deferred in systematic differentiation until hermeneutics turns the achievement of language around toward its metaphorical origin.

The hermeneutical exigency as we have defined it is not felt until language reveals itself as forgetful of the forces it has brought to meaning. What is first sometimes thought to be a loss of meaning is better described as a loss of the meaning of meaning. That is, when language does not see itself mirrored as a metaphorical achievement, it becomes flattened in a horizontal semantic display. It is dazzled by the complexity of what is present and forgets that the presence reveals an absence. The loss of that sense of absence negates consciousness of the achievement of language as a transformation of force into meaning.

The sense of absence attends every experience of language. The hermeneutical exigency is satisfied in the consciousness of the sound of silence and the presence of absence. It is this consciousness that is at once both hermeneutical and theological. The lucid metaphor appears and is attended to in the radical questions of hermeneutical thinking that can be descriptively characterized as an accession to theological language or the theological use of language. Not only is the language of a wholly other absence often part of a theological lexicon, but to entertain unconditional questions also is itself to do theological inquiry. Theology can push language to limits of intelligibility where ordinary meanings are prophetically negated or parabolically reversed.

There are two transgressions. When concepts transgress the limits of intelligibility in extreme formulations, their meaning disappears. We are then conscious not of the presence of meaning but of the disappearance of meaning into an absence that now is itself only a memory. The other transgression is to turn language on itself in a parabolic reversal that wounds established external meanings. This self-referential moment is a display of the metaphoricity of language. When language turns on itself, it encounters a presence that is no more than itself. The parabolic reversal is an acute consciousness of absence. The metaphor gains in lucidity. Meaning is brought closer to force by the recognition of what language is and what it is not. In act and content this recognition is a theological affirmation, because in all its expressions it intends the theological silence that is both absent and other than itself.

Force is a reality other than language.[19] Consciousness thus transcends the achievement of its own linguistic display in the struggle for origination. This wrestling with unnamed demons may issue forth in theological meaning, but it is first of all an experience of transcendence that is religious. The postcritical text is now also in its fresh statement a precritical text. The theological and hermeneutical exigencies have led us to force and thereby to religion.

Theology is not force and theology is not religion. Theology is writing and writing is repression. Unless it becomes silent, theology can always return to the book, to writing. Theology is a pretext. Its hermeneutical achievement is a text that exists prior to the text of religious experience. Its visible achievement is writing; but this is a pretext. It is only when we know that it is a pretext that we know about its work and at the same time know that its work is not what it is about.

NOTES

1. Edmund Jabès, *The Book of Questions* (Middletown, Conn.: Wesleyan Univ. Press, 1976), 13.

2. Hans-Georg Gadamer, *Truth and Method* (New York: Seabury Press, 1975), 354.

3. Anika Lemaire, *Jacques Lacan* (London: Henley; Boston: Routledge & Kegan Paul, 1979), 51.

4. Jacques Derrida, *Speech and Phenomena* (Evanston, Ill.: Northwestern Univ. Press, 1973), 129–30.

5. Jacques Derrida, *Writing and Difference* (Chicago: Univ. of Chicago Press, 1978), 211.

6. Harold Bloom, *The Anxiety of Influence: A Theory of Poetry* (New York: Oxford Univ. Press, 1973), 5–16.

7. Ibid., 13.

8. Ibid., 5.

9. Michel Foucault, *Language, Counter-Memory, Practice* (Ithaca, N.Y.: Cornell Univ. Press, 1977), 42.

10. Ibid., 14.

11. Paul Ricoeur, *Freud and Philosophy: An Essay on Interpretation* (New Haven, Conn.: Yale Univ. Press, 1970), 384.

12. Thomas J. J. Altizer, *The Self-Embodiment of God* (New York: Harper & Row, 1977), 4.

13. Ibid., 16.

14. Thomas J. J. Altizer, *Total Presence: The Language of Jesus and the Language of Today* (New York: Seabury Press, 1980), 99.

15. Foucault, *Language, Counter-Memory, Practice*, 55.

16. Derrida, *Speech and Phenomena*, 41.

17. Ibid.

18. Paul Ricoeur, *The Conflict of Interpretations* (Evanston, Ill.: Northwestern Univ. Press, 1974), 65.

19. Derrida, *Writing and Difference*, 27.

5

Body, Text and Imagination

God is a questioning of God.—Reb Arwas
—Edmund Jabès, *The Book of Questions*

In 1896 Freud published a paper examining the etiology of neuroses in which he first used the word psychoanalysis to describe a method of investigation that inaugurated discursive patterns marking the beginning of a trail into an imaginal reality and imaginal body.

> Travelling backwards into the patient's past, and always guided by the organic train of symptoms and of memories and thoughts aroused, I finally reached the starting point of the pathological process; and I was obliged to see that at bottom the same thing was present in all the cases submitted to analysis—the action of an agent which must be accepted as the specific cause of hysteria. . . . The event of which the subject has retained an unconscious memory is a *precocious experience of sexual relations with actual excitement of the genitals, resulting from sexual abuse committed by another person.*[1]

In 1897 Freud wrote a letter to Wilhelm Fliess in which he confessed, "I no longer believe in my *neurotica.*"[2] It was the necessary action of the agent, the event with *actual* excitement of the genitals, that he no longer believed in.

> It is curious that I feel not in the least disgraced, though the occasion might seem to require it. Certainly I shall not tell it in Gath, or publish it in the streets of Askalon, in the land of the Philistines—but between ourselves I have a feeling more of triumph than of defeat (which cannot be right).[3]

That curious sense of triumph accompanied a further step toward the recognition of the text of the imaginal body.

In 1918 Freud published the case history of the "Wolf Man." Through a dazzling display of analytical virtuosity he uncovers a primal scene at the heart of this obsessional neurosis. He then says:

> I should myself be glad to know whether the primal scene in my present patient's case was a phantasy or a real experience; but, taking other similar cases into account, I must admit that the answer to this question is not in fact a matter of very great importance.[4]

A very important development occurred in psychoanalytic discourse between the paper of 1896 and the publication of the case history of the "Wolf Man." Freud deepened his grasp of the textuality of psychological experience and expanded the boundaries of what was psychoanalytically possible to say. The body expressed itself in the text of memory and the text became its own body. It mattered less and less whether the experience of the body of the text was historically congruent with the experience of the physical body. It was the image of the body, the imaginal body, the body of the text that was the prime material constructed and transformed by healing psychoanalytical narrative. Freud experientially deconstructed the epistemological frame holding the metaphor of language as the mirror of nature. It is probably his self-analysis that cleared space for an interpretation of dreams as a paradigm for cultural representation that is always subject to disguise, distortion, displacement, and stereotyped symbolization. The base material, the text of the phenomenal world, is given as an impure text representing the body.

Psychoanalysis began as a "talking cure." It began with a text and not with a *tabula rasa*. The markings on the given tablet are always of an uncertain origin because they do not materially correspond with what they represent. The markings are present, and that presence announces an absence of what is represented that is also a difference from what is represented. What Freud discovered in his fantasies and in the fantasies of his patients was a crisis in our relationship to language. Language was not a mirror of nature that established an identity. It was a reduplication of nature that established a difference. Words can be objects but they are not the objects they represent. It is in the gap defined by this difference that Freud delivered a wound to the light-metaphors of consciousness and the mirror-metaphors of language.

Freud is not the only philosopher of suspicion that has delivered a wound to the root metaphors of western epistemology. Marx and Nietzsche are often cited for their contribution to this philosophical upheaval, and recently Richard Rorty has elegantly argued that the epistemic privilege of mirror images has been laid waste in the Anglo-American tradition and that it is time for a philosophy without mirrors, a move from epistemology to hermeneutics.[5] Although the wound inflicted on consciousness and language is not a singular achievement of Freud, it is especially interesting in Freud because he senses a triumph in inflicting the wound to his own theory. More important, he stays with the body and the sexual etiology of the neuroses. What is changed is the body. It is the reduplicated body of the text that is important and subject to psychoanalytic augmentation and intervention. The body of the text is a subtle body, metaphorical and polymorphic. Possibly it is this new body that Freud was sensing in his affirmation to Fliess. The metaphorical construction of the body in a semantics of meaning is not limited to physiological possibilities or historical probabilities. Its importance and sexuality can be disseminated throughout the whole semantic realm by word play in a system of intertextual references. The signifier was freed from its biological limitations. What was sexual could become psychosexual and what became psychosexual could become all of culture through a linguistic imperialism mobilized by concepts of defense and sublimation. These concepts, as was pointed out in the earlier reference to Harold Bloom, correspond to rhetorical tropes.[6] Freud cleared semantic space by his map of misreading for the dissemination of the body throughout the whole of culture.

The shattering of the mirror of language denies a privileged representation of the body in a semantic field, but it does not deny the representation of the body that is a reduplication. This body, however, is not limited and is not always recognizable as body. It is this body that Freud extended into all cultural achievements and that I am identifying as the body of the text. It is not just the text but the sensuality of the text that is its subtle body. Since the body that is represented falls outside of its representation, the subtle body of the text is a presence of what is absent. Its sensuality depends on that presence and its subtlety on the absence. We are talking about two bodies and one body. Their relationship is part of the enigma of our beginning.

The two bodies are not identical but there is a play between them, and because of that playful dialectic we sense a unity that is always appearing and disappearing. Our beginning is an act and not a text, but it is an act that appears only in the text. We are restricted to the text because it is what appears in the assignment of meaning to the play. The play of meaning in a language game is a familiar metaphor since Wittgenstein introduced this concept in his *Philosophical Investigations.* "Here the term 'language-*game*' is meant to bring into prominence the fact that the speaking of language is part of an activity, or a form of life."[7] He later says that "the meaning of a word is its use in language."[8] The activity, the form of life, the use in language all seem closer to our experience of textuality than the mirror image of the world or ourselves. The mirror has no support or meaning outside the language game.

The semantic achievement is not perceptual. Only if we stood in close proximity to objects as we were naming them and accompanied the naming with a pointing gesture might we sustain the metaphor of the mirror image. As soon as we distance ourselves and defer the meaning, we immediately note a difference. The deferring is a differing. We are playing a game that is not governed by the primacy of perception. The rules that govern the game are the rules of discourse. Perception notes a discontinuity through the deferral. The word *dog* does not look like a dog, sound like a dog, or feel like a dog. The semantic *dog* is accessible to a whole world of meanings; it is pliable; it can be transformed. This accession into language can be a multiplication of meaning but it is also a loss of the presence of the dog in the economy of its world of natural forces. All our talk about the dog has been a transformation of force into meaning. We mark a difference not at the beginning but in the deferral.

We should not, however, think that we can recover an identity with experience that is not already different from itself, because every return is but another deferral. We can only throw a fleeting glance at a beginning through the theater of memory already burdened with the multiplication of meanings. We find meaning when we search for force, but this repetition of meaning within the game may be a clue to the beginning that eludes our grasp. That is, the search for a beginning is the repetition of the beginning. We constantly try to repeat life in a more accessible form.[9] Once again we cannot grasp the beginning, so we *begin* the search for the beginning.

When we are awash with meanings, we experience the absence of our achievement. Our achievement is the repression of force. The language game is the substitution of a cultural world of meanings, controlled and accessible, for the lost, seething, tumbling disorder of forces that molest our memories. Language can only tell the tale of the origination of its speech in the space of its achievement; and there it simply marks an absence. That is, its mark is an absence of the force it represents.

We see this activity writ small in a story Freud relates about a small boy of 1 1/2 years.[10] The boy could say only a few comprehensible words and make a few sounds intelligible to those around him. He was a good little boy except for a habit of throwing his toys away from him. He made a sound as he threw his toys away that both Freud and the boy's mother thought represented the German word *fort* (gone). Freud said he later noticed that the boy played a game with a wooden reel and a string. He would throw the reel and make a sound that approximated *fort.* After the reel disappeared he would pull the string until it returned and say *da* (there). The child found great satisfaction in this game of *fort:da.* It was a game that reduplicated and repeated the theme of disappearance and return.

> The interpretation of the game then became obvious. It was related to the child's great cultural achievement—the instinctual renunciation [that is, the renunciation of instinctual satisfaction] which he had made in allowing his mother to go away without protesting. He compensated himself for this, as it were, by himself staging the disappearance and return of the objects within his reach.[11]

The little boy gained mastery over the turbulent forces that accompanied the temporary loss of his mother by reduplicating the loss in a game that had rules guaranteeing the return of the lost object.

Freud used this illustration to talk about the motives that lead children to play. He thought most theories up to this time failed to bring the *economic* motive to the foreground. A yield of pleasure accompanies the play.[12] The aesthetics of play is complemented by this economic consideration. *Fort:da* reduplicates rather than mirrors the disappearance:appearance of the mother so that the child has control over his created world and receives pleasure from it. The game is overdetermined in the realm of force, but not in the realm of forces that determine the mother's behavior. There is a sensuality in the text of the child's game, but because of the real absence of the mother it should be clear that "the pleasure of the text is irreducible to physiological need."[13] Physiological needs are woven through the spaces of the text in the satisfaction of mixed discourse so that this satisfaction is not simply semantic or economic. The satisfaction is a dialectical achievement approximated in the appearance of the text before it disappears behind the materiality of the text.

The dialectic is a double loss and a double gain, and the sensuality of the text that is its satisfaction lies in the breaches constituted by the complexity of these multiple actions. The first loss corresponds with the first gain. A signifier in the semantic realm is substituted for a force in our physiological or physical economy. The loss or repression of force in this substitution is at the same time a gain in meaning—a semantic connectedness. The reel and string are substituted for the mother. The word is substituted for the body. The reel and string are subject to the laws of *fort:da.* Mastery and meaning can be found in the game, but the game itself corresponds with the loss or disappearance of the mother.

Freud does not say, but it can be easily imagined from our own experiences, that the satisfaction in the production of meaning in the game could be great enough that even when the mother reappears it could go on and her reappearance could now be an intrusion. Many of us have held onto the seduction of the subtle body of the text to the exclusion of the physiological body. In fact, even my talk of the physiological body is already a representation and a repression.

This enigma is an aspect of the second loss and gain that are together a coincidental antinomy with the first loss and gain. The appearance of the text is the display or the gain of a new materiality. That is, the text has an ontic status. It stands materially in the realm of force, and this materiality is not contained in the meaning that is the first gain in the transformation of force into meaning. The presence of meaning requiring the materiality of the text, sound or inscription, has in its representation of what is now absent established a new presence in the economy of forces that is itself not represented in the semantics of meaning. The text can never exhaust its potential for meaning through multiplication or repetition: it always establishes a material presence that eludes the range of what is immediately reduplicated, because this immediate presence lies in the realm of an economics of force. The materiality or fabric of the text is a sensuous weave precisely because it is never what it appears to be. It never contains itself.

There is something uncanny about the text. We are used to the first experience of gain and loss. Through it we create a world that is intelligible. It is a world that can be mastered, repeated, and expanded. But as we travel through this created world sometimes we miss a connection, and much like a traveler left sitting in a train station, we note the detailed materiality of what is around us. If it is a long wait, the walls, the chairs, the doors, the scattered newspapers, everything becomes oppressive in its presence. It doesn't fit into a narrative. We missed a connection: suddenly we have to account for what appears and not what it means. This material reflexivity presses in on us whenever we miss a connection. The waiting is a beginning. We feel that we have to make sense of the materiality of the text.

Artists, poets, and novelists disturb the popular imagination when their work becomes materially reflexive. When the text becomes a reflection on textuality, when painting or sculpture presents its medium as its subject rather than represents what it is not, there is a representation of secondary gain and loss. The paradox is that the missed connection becomes the first connection to a new repression of force and proliferation of meaning. What defies our expectation is that we cannot go back to the first text after we have missed a connection. The supplement that comes out of this breach has altered the economy of forces that was represented in the first text. The supplement transgresses the first text and is irreducible to it since the supplement has its own originality. We know of no absolute text that lies behind present texts. All we know are present texts, and all that we can say lies behind a text is the scene of its origination. That scene can only be represented in a new text. Even if we think we are getting behind a text, we are not at the same time getting behind textuality.

Secondary loss and gain can be illustrated simply in Freud's example of the *fort:da* game. The gain in control and meaning in substitution of the reel and string for the loss of the mother is supplemented by the material instrumentality of the reel and string. The reel and string are the material possibility for the representational substitution and mastery of *fort:da* in controlling the meaning of the disappearance:appearance of the mother. There is a gain in meaning and control but also a gain in materiality that is a loss of meaning and control. The game works as long as the string does not break, the reel remains tied to the string, or there are no obstacles to the retrieval of the reel. The materiality of the text of this game introduces a different set of forces from those mastered in compensation for the disappearance of the mother.

The game repeats life in a more accessible form for the child, and all works well until the string breaks. The broken string would be a missed connection that halts the flow of meaning. The first experience of the child would not be fresh display of new meanings but a grief over the loss of meaning. The forces that control the action of the reel and string are not meaningful in the text of *fort:da*. The break of the string and the breach of the text would be an intrusion of what are again untamed forces. The text would remain overdetermined in an economics of force, but pleasure would give way to anger and anxiety. The attention of the child would be focused on the materiality of the reel and string and not on the meaning generated in the game. Probably anger would be directed toward the broken object and then anxiety would surround the broken text.

The double determination, the double gain, and the double loss are the risks that accompany every game and every text. No text can be complete and authorized: it is always more than it appears. No text can be exhaustively true, and every text is sensual. Texts cannot escape their materiality. This is a part of the text that is opaque. The double determination also means that there are at least two edges to the text. The text is duplex. It speaks a duplicity. When connections are missed the seams in the fabric of the text show. Sometimes the surface garment gapes and we witness the sensuous surface of the text. These moments are not themselves filled with meaning but constitute the loss of meaning and space for meaning. The commitment to understanding the givenness of experience places us before these appearances. We do not here have a foundation, but we do have a beginning. The saving of the appearances is a saving of the text/image, or we might even say a saving of the imagination. We must talk about the imagination because the text is never only literal. It is event as well as content. There is a scene of origination, and as much as we might want to get behind that scene to a foundation we have to take account of the scene if we are honest to experience.

What appears in language is not nature but the text. The text is not a mirror but a supplement. It has its own presence that breaks with nature, draws away from nature, and establishes its own meaning. This is what is meant by a scene of origination.[14] The very existence of words indicates "a breach with the phenomenality of things."[15] We cannot turn to nature to give an account of the scene of textual origination, because the presence of the text is a break or breach that moves away from nature. We also cannot turn to semantics to tell us about the scene of textual origination, because the functional relations internal to the text refer only to themselves. The scene is event-ful. The scene is part of a theater. Telling must be also showing, because it is not just the appearance of the text but the appearing of the text that constitutes the scene.

In Freud, the scene of origination, the primal scene, is a repression that at the same time creates and compromises culture. The diachronic fantasy of societal origins is reduplicated in particularized histories of individuals as an axial reference in the further dissemination of their textual identity. For Derrida, Freud's primal scene, the breach with nature, is a scene of writing.

> In that moment of world history "subsumed" by the name of Freud, by means of an unbelievable mythology ... a relationship to itself of the historico-transcendental stage of writing was spoken without being said, thought without being thought: was written and simultaneously erased, metaphorized; designating itself while indicating intraworldly relations, it was represented.[16]

Bloom gives priority to the trespass of teaching, a scheme of transumption or metaleptic reversal that he calls the primal scene of instruction.[17]

The primal scene is itself the trope of a trope. It is the re-presentation of representation. It doubles the imagination by imagining imagination. Figures for the transgression of language are substituted for the transgression of nature. The assault on language is a reduplication of the assault on nature. The substitution of the reel and string for the disappearing mother is brought to immediate awareness by the choice to break the string. The break with nature was the substitution of the reel and string for the mother. The way back to the substitution is by transgression of the game, breaking the string. The broken figure sacrifices meaning in an attempt to represent the origination of meaning. Meaning is brought to force, gives recognition to force, but does not itself become force.

The entertainment of troped language approximates a mixed discourse in a semantic display. It references the transformation of experience through the dialectic of presence and absence that makes it no longer identical with itself. The primal scene is always a metaphor. A scene is substituted for an act of disjunction between force and meaning, just as within that act meaning is substituted for force. A scene of substitution is substituted for an act of substitution. There is both a reenactment and a reduplication. Here is a dialectic that is the foundation of mixed discourse. This dialectic is neither language nor force but is rooted in force and spread throughout language. The dialectic does not take us behind or below metaphor. It is a delineation of what we mean by metaphor.

This is an expanded view of metaphor that turns to discourse instead of the word or sentence for the unit of determination. The use of metaphor can be a rhetorical strategy within discourse, but more important, it is the possibility for discourse. Discourse is mimetic of its foundation when it creates meaning through internal substitutions of dissimilar units of nomination. Discourse is itself the substitution of words for forces. This is why discourse is always mixed and indeterminate. A necessary ambiguity lies in the wake of discursive achievements because of their metaphorical structure. Literalism is an illusion. What we mean by meaning requires both substitution and difference. To give meaning to an experience is to alter the experience through primary and secondary loss and gain. For example, *putting* something into words and *putting* something into type are progressive substitutions that are determinate only by their own presence. Only if language were a mirror and discourse a mirroring could we posit a literalism. Discourse is the dialectical work of a metaphorical movement. It makes a difference. We are makers of meaning.

There is tension in this insight. The making of meaning is at the same time a loss. Force is repressed as force in order to become accessible as meaning. Meaning is both an achievement and an alienation. We have recognized here that the world of meaning is a mediated achievement amidst immediate forces. Life hangs over the gap between meaning and force. It is in the space of this gap that we sense a surplus of meaning or metaphorical potential for the further determination of meaning. It is also in the space of this gap that there is room for the return of the repressed. Discourse continually passes through this space, but the direction of its movement is variable. The metaphorical potential of discourse allows it to move from force to meaning or to bring meaning to force. These are different movements and not simply a change in direction. The creation of meaning is a repression through active substitution. The movement of meaning to force is not a substitution but a subversion of language achievements made possible because of secondary gains in the creation of meaning. The subversion is a deconstruction of the material instrumentality needed for the substitution for making meaning. We can subvert the game of *fort:da* by breaking the string that connects to the reel. We can subvert a language game by troping the conventional patterns that hold together its disparate parts. There is no single or ideal task for discourse. Each discipline of the imagination will have to create a genre of mixed discourse to fulfill its metaphorical potential and to determine the direction of its movement.

The history of every imaginal discipline will be a history of movements: starts, false starts, grand journeys, and reversals. Usually only at times of crisis is there an awareness that the metaphorical potential of discourse is indeterminate. When movement slows or is paralyzed, a reversal of former movements is possible. The discipline hesitates in recognition of the ambiguity of its own possibilities. The crisis that ensues is usually thought to be a crisis of meaning or values that reside in particular patterns of meaning, when in fact what we are experiencing is a larger crisis in our relationship with language. Discourse is mixed and has only one of its feet planted in the realm of semantic achievement. When the semantic achievement falters the crisis has begun, but we have not plumbed its depths if we restrict our thinking to the problem of meaning. Deconstruction is as important a movement as reconstruction. The problem in assessing the range of possible movements, of course, is that discourse cannot simply reverse itself and talk in the economics of force. It speaks and writes in the semantic realm of meanings. It faces the semantic realm.

Deconstruction is dizzying. It is a walking backward. It is a subversion that is hard to sustain, because at the same time it is disseminating a new speech that can be multiplied and repeated in the construction of meaning. Of course, a contrasting predominantly constructive orientation also evidences the deconstruction of precursor figures and figurations. In deconstructionist thought it is the dominance of a negative capability that distinguishes it from self-consciously constructive thinking. Deconstructive discourse is depressive. It pulls the semantic achievement down toward what was repressed by the very fact of representational origination. The new speech it disseminates is usually a metalanguage that firms its footing in the semantic realm, because the foot placed in the semantically indeterminate realm of force can never be sure of itself.

Deconstructionist thought has deep roots in philosophical, structuralist, and psychoanalytic sensitivities, but in America it is best known and practiced in literary-critical circles. There was already a tradition of structuralist criticism, and since "the saving of the text" is a fundamental theme of deconstruction the immediate application to literary criticism is obvious. However, the work of deconstructionist literary critics has become very important for understanding the work of all disciplines with texts. The shattering of language as the mirror of nature, insight into the metaphoricity of all discourse, and other legacies of deconstructionism alter what most imaginative disciplines understand as their foundation. Their work cannot proceed as if untouched on a deep level when the materiality of texts becomes an impassable passage and the text is at the heart of the discipline. The aporetic opacity of texts clearly affects the work of theologians, philosophers, and social scientists. It is not a problem that can be put aside as somebody else's. The intertwining of body, text, and imagination in the mask of culture is a problem for thinking that is as universal as the cultural disguise that covers our world. We need to think this problem through in many disciplines to experience its importance.

The deconstructionist problem is not the creation of one group of thinkers. It is the problem of the text: its origin in discourse and writing, the materiality of its presence, and its relationship to the realities it represents. These are persistent problems that have been well documented in the histories of philosophy and theology. They emerge whenever thinking turns on itself and experiences its textual supplement. Deconstructionism did not create the problem, but it displays a new discursivity that can generate a literature that is yet untried in much philosophical and theological thinking or in the social sciences.

Theology is a particularly interesting discipline to look at in relationship to deconstructionist themes, because it has clearly witnessed a crisis in its relationship with language. The ferment in theology from the early sixties on has been a persistent discussion of the possibility for theological language. The question that has occupied the center of theological reflection over the past two decades does not center on the validity of theological language but the meaning or meaninglessness of theological language. Theology has questioned its own possibility. Perhaps it should have questioned whether it had anything interesting to say.

The eclipse of God, the disappearance of God, and the death of God became serious discussions when the material instrumentality of theological discourse was experienced as disconnected from any reference in the real world. In 1969, Langdon Gilkey retrospectively asserted that the fundamental question being asked by the new theologians was a very different question from those asked by their liberal and neo-orthodox teachers. "Is there in experience any transcendent dimension for which religious or theological language is necessary and in relation to which it makes sense?"[18] That question in its various forms of expression had the power to break the literal connection of theology with the world it had claimed to represent.

The missed connection, the broken string, and the death of God coalesce in this image and bring to our mind the deconstructionist reminder of the materiality of the text. The child's game of *fort:da* mastering the disappearance of the mother uncomfortably parallels the theological language game mastering the disappearance of God. What is important is that both games take on a new significance when the string is broken or a connection is missed.

Theology must stop and look around at its own semantic achievement when experience can no longer sustain the literal connection between theology's words and the world it represents. Theology is not a mirror. It is writing, and writing is a substitution and a repression. Theology represents a world, but the connection is not literal. As in other disciplines of the imagination, its scene of origination is metaphorical. Perhaps theology always knew it was metaphorical as it led readers through the labyrinth of a dark night of the soul, or up the sides of magical mountains, or into the complexities of an inner verbum. Maybe it always disguised its second order of reflection in the first-order display of the world it claimed to represent or even present. Now, after inflicting wounds on itself, it must take account of the semantic achievement that is its construction.

The emphasis on construction in theology immediately comes up against the metaphor of deconstruction. Its texts are rich and varied. Theology has not restricted its questions or limited the domain of its inquiry. Even after its confrontation with meaninglessness, it continues to talk of transcendence, ultimate horizons, and eschatological disclosures. It continues to construct worlds under horizons of hope, freedom, and love. Sometimes it rewrites history as a prolepsis of apocalyptic happenings. It talks not only of presence but of total presence. In general it now self-consciously constructs a world using a limit-language.

Gordon Kaufman, in *An Essay on Theological Method,* writes:

Theology ... is fundamentally an activity of *construction* (and reconstruction) not of description or exposition, as it has been ordinarily understood in the past; and the failure to grasp this fact has led to mistaken expectations for theology and to the use of misleading criteria both in doing theology and in assessing its conclusions.[19]

He says that when we recognize theology as a constructive activity, "it becomes clear that the central problem of theological method is to discern and formulate explicit criteria and procedures for theological construction."[20] How does this assertion of the central methodological problem of theology relate to deconstructionism? This is not an isolated question to be directed to Kaufman's work alone. Serious postcritical theologies have generally acknowledged the overdetermination of meaning and the function of the imagination in theological construction. They have accepted responsibility for making meaning in theological thinking. Philosophical hermeneutics has helped shape a theopoetic sensibility that has revitalized traditional theological work. Theology has rescued itself from the museum through a meta-analysis of the second order that has saved the text from an incredulous literalism and for imaginative construction. Second-order theology is a multiplication of meaning that returns the text to the work of theology.

The work is still to be done. Kaufman is again very helpful in locating the problem by calling for us to "recognize both the possibility and appropriateness of a third-order theology."[21]

> That is, acknowledging that all theological positions are rooted fundamentally in imaginative construction (second-order theology), we must now take control (so far as possible) of our theological activity and attempt deliberately to construct our concepts and images of God and the world; and then we must seek to see human existence in terms of these symbolical constructions.[22]

If deconstructionism is to have a place in theology, it will be in this third order, yet to be determined. Now placed before us is the decision how to take control of the theological task. At first glance, deconstructionist thinking would reverse the direction suggested by Kaufman; but we must remind ourselves of the complex dialectic of metaphorical loss and gain before we harden this assessment. Deconstructionist thinking should be examined as an available option for third-order theology even when the task is first envisioned as a constructive task.

Third-order theology begins with the textual legacy of first- and second-order theologies. How do we *take control* of our activity in the midst of the texts that constitute this legacy? How do we choose to stand in relationship to these texts? How do we do theology in this crowded marketplace of established meanings?

Whatever else may characterize third-order theology, we know that it will be a hermeneutic of texts. Otherwise it would be of the first or second orders. The problem of starting is deciding what we do following the postcritical relinquishment of descriptive literalism. The experience of the text and textuality block even sophisticated appeals to romantic primitivisms with attendant literalisms that call us back to the Bible, back to nature, or back to origins. These are all too easily seen as diachronic fantasies elaborated from textual achievements to be taken seriously as an escape from the responsibility of third-order theology. What we see is that instead of the text taking us behind itself, it expands. A new text then confronts us that supplements our beginning reflection, and we are again faced with the question of how to do theology.

The problem of how to begin a third-order theology is clearer when we acknowledge that second-order theology is a permanent dislocation of the dreams of Enlightenment rationalism for a replication of nature in the mirror of language, and this is not a wound that can be healed. The dream has been dislocated from the center of thinking. It is one dream beside others. We begin with metaphor, talk about metaphor metaphorically, and recognize every closure as a metaphorical achievement. Third-order theology must be self-consciously a mixed discourse. Its beginning is fluid. The texts cannot dictate our response. That is, the work lies between the spaces of past achievements, and how we move is not yet determined. This is why we can talk about taking control of theological activity. There is a tension in every metaphor, a conflict in every interpretation, and a conflict between interpretations.

We are in a privileged space of overdetermination touching both force and meaning. It is a hermeneutical field. The achievements are duplex and show themselves in their duplicity. As Paul Ricoeur has shown, we can work expansively toward the recollection and restoration of meaning,[23] or we can shape interpretation as an exercise of suspicion.[24] Both moves can work within the metaphoricity of language, and both moves recognize the mythopoetic core of the imagination.

The hermeneutics of expansion is an exegetical work. It repeats the text and multiplies its meaning in a supplementary expansion throughout the semantic realm. This is the option Kaufman describes when he suggests we construct concepts and images of God and the world and then disseminate them broadly so that we see human existence in relationship to these constructions. In contrast, the hermeneutics of suspicion is transgressive. It violates the text by forcing it back on its materiality, by perforating its surface achievement with questions that direct us to what the text is not, by troping patterns of internal coherence, and by stretching connections to the breaking point.

The hermeneutics of expansion recognizes in the metaphoricity of discourse the opportunity for unrestricted elaboration in the semantic realm. Every text can be lifted into a more complex pattern of meaning or re-collected under a larger horizon. Theology can become a phenomenology of the spirit "in which each figure finds its meaning, not in what precedes but in what follows."[25] Theology can elaborate the subtle body of the text so that it envelops the semantic world. Once language is no longer viewed as a mirror of nature, there are only internal controls on definitional complexity. A lexical hierarchy can be generated by progressive substitution and repression until an all-encompassing concept of "that than which nothing greater can be conceived" stands abstractly in relationship to all other concepts and images. God can be created semantically through metaphorical gain. We might even say that the concept of God is the teleological fulfillment of the metaphorical potential in discourse. "God is a questioning of God."

The deconstruction within a hermeneutics of suspicion is also a discursive achievement. It creates a supplementary text, but this text transgresses rather than augments the meaning of received texts. Patterns of interference create spaces in and between the texts, and the spaces are more highly valued than the text. Spaces isolate texts and cast them adrift on the sea of forces. Language is sometimes contracted or condensed so that the supplementary text intends silence. Rhetorical tropes are combined to hide connections and force the textual images to stand in front of us by themselves in a space cleared by disguise. The missed connections delay representation and the material presence of the image is mute.

The semantic activity in deconstructionist discourse is variable and always particular. Language can be pushed so far that it transgresses the limits of intelligibility, meaning disappears, and we are left with the materiality of speech or writing. The elision of principal parts of ordinary discourse hints at the achievement of meaning but again only displays the materiality of discourse. The introduction of dissimilar constructions into narrative progressions stops the expected flow, turns discourse, and clears the space where we had anticipated the establishment of meaning. The collision or overlay of dissimilar texts will often cancel out parts, isolate images that claim our attention, and draw us into their extralinguistic isolation. Graphological displacements can also subvert the flow of meaning and leave us with a naked text.

Deconstructionist thought explicitly or implicitly interrogates the text. The different styles of inquiry all establish a practical method for attending to the importance of questions that violate the semantic framework in which they are enclosed. This violation is a recognition at the same time of language as naturally symbolic and of discourse as the path between meaning and force. We can cross the path in either direction.

Deconstructionist theological discourse tries to pull back the text toward the economics of force. It is a depressive movement that subverts the horizontal semantic display. It is a constant reminder of the metaphor that gives textual body to physical body. We step back into the forces of the imagination as we prescind from its achievement.

Third-order theological construction can be incorporated into deconstructionist theology's agenda along with first- and second-order semantic achievements. Even deconstructionism's own textual achievement is subject to further work. It continually reverses the semantic flow and folds language back on itself. The text is a momentary closure, and the text can always be deconstructed. The project has no closure. Representation always announces an absence. The most elaborate theological constructions are empty of everything but their own material presence. Theological constructions need the deconstruction that pulls them back toward the economics of force. They must be plumbed constantly for their metaphorical roots if they are to remain fecund. "God is a questioning of God" is interesting because it represents an absence, has a mute sensuality, and represents the transcendence of a body of experience. Deconstruction gives significance to meaning.

Construction and deconstruction are complementary but not co-incidental strategies of third-order theology. They work with texts and disseminate texts that constitute the body of subjective experience. Together they intertwine force and meaning so that experiencing their complementarity is not a task to be carried to resolution. There is no resolution. There is instead a tension and a complex dialectic that, when it is represented, is a reduplication of the metaphoricity of language. A unified search for the meaning of third-order theology would require a reductionist interpretation that forgets its metaphorical beginnings and represses the economics of force. The simple proliferation of texts will establish meanings. These meanings will have to be allowed to interfere with each other as part of a dialectical interchange between force and meaning. The interchange works because of textual and intertextual absences in the semantic realm.

Every text can be elaborated and transgressed. Every text is a pre-text in relationship to future texts and at the same time the residue of the scene of its origination. However the text is taken up in future discourse, it brings with it a meaning that is the work of repression and substitution.

As we deepen our grasp on the textuality of theological experience and expand the boundaries of what it is theologically possible to say, we, like Freud, will work with the subtle body of the text as a substitute for the text of the body. We cannot escape the deferral of desire in the scene of origination.

NOTES

1. Sigmund Freud, *The Standard Edition of the Complete Psychological Works of Sigmund Freud,* 24 vols. (London: Hogarth Press and the Institute of Psychoanalysis, 1953–74), 3:151–52 (hereafter cited as SE).

2. Sigmund Freud, *The Origins of Psychoanalysis: The Letters to Wilhelm Fliess* (New York: Basic Books, 1954), 215.

3. Ibid., 217.

4. SE 17:97.

5. Cf. Richard Rorty, *Philosophy and the Mirror of Nature* (Princeton: Princeton Univ. Press, 1979).

6. Harold Bloom, *A Map of Misreading* (New York: Oxford Univ. Press, 1975), 84.

7. Ludwig Wittgenstein, *Philosophical Investigations* (Oxford: Basil Blackwell & Mott, 1967), 11

8. Ibid., 20.

9. Cf. Edward Said, *Beginnings: Intention and Method* (Baltimore: Johns Hopkins Univ. Press, 1975), 89.

10. SE 18:14–17.

11. Ibid., 14.

12. Ibid.

13. Roland Barthes, *The Pleasure of the Text* (New York: Hill & Wang, 1975), 17.

14. Jacques Derrida, *Of Grammatology* (Baltimore: Johns Hopkins Univ. Press, 1974), 151.

15. Geoffrey H. Hartman, *Saving the Text* (Baltimore: Johns Hopkins Univ. Press, 1981), xvi.

16. Jacques Derrida, *Writing and Difference* (Chicago: Univ. of Chicago Press, 1978), 228–29.

17. Bloom, *Map of Misreading,* 32, 49.

18. Langdon Gilkey, *Naming the Whirlwind: The Renewal of God-Language* (Indianapolis: Bobbs-Merrill, 1969), 13.

19. Gordon D. Kaufman, *An Essay on Theological Method* (Missoula, Mont.: Scholars Press, 1979), x.

20. Ibid., 36.

21. Ibid., 38.

22. Ibid.

23. Paul Ricoeur, *Freud and Philosophy: An Essay on Interpretation* (New Haven: Yale Univ. Press, 1970), 28–32.

24. Ibid., 32–36.

25. Paul Ricoeur, *The Conflict of Interpretations* (Evanston, Ill.: Northwestern Univ. Press, 1974), 21.

6

Theology and the Public Body

The characteristics we have ascribed to theological thinking alter the understanding of the public character of theology. The question needs to be raised how we position the practice of radical theological thinking as a discursive activity in the midst of a public body of experience. It is part of a social drama, and the social drama can receive theological thinking into itself only in a way consonant with the internal constitution of theological thinking.

It is clear from earlier chapters that when we begin to characterize theological thinking we must begin with the recognition that theology is writing. Theology is the written product of theological thinking and discourse. The materiality of the theological text is an important element in positioning theological reflection because it is a part of theological reflection. It is something to be read, heard, or thought. It is always more than what it is in its material presence, and this is what we need to understand when we place theology in a theory of practice. We need a deconstruction in theology to see how theological discourses are constructed so we can assess the practice of theology with regard to the range of its effective action.

Prior to such a deconstruction there are several statements we can make about theology that help map the terrain of our inquiry. There are family resemblances among genres of symbolic action, and these are open to general inquiry that can be thematized and articulated to form the interior limits of inquiry for which any specific critique of a discipline is responsible. A specific critique is responsible to questions no less far ranging than the questions posed by the general inquiry. The general inquiry can set the tone for a specific critique and guard against its premature closure.

The first thing we can say about theology to place it in a general context is that it has to do with words. "Whatever else it may be, and wholly regardless of whether it be true or false, theology is preeminently verbal."[1] Theology is formally a discursive act in the privacy of an interior soliloquy or in the drama of public reflexivity. It exists as a voice or a text that is spoken or written, heard or read. We speak to be heard even if we intend ourselves to be the single auditor. There may be private moments of speech but there is no private language. The code is collective and public. Meaning is in principle a public affair. It is a semantic achievement and is established in a semantic field or domain that is structurally and historically collective.

To position theology we have to account for its public reflexivity, because it is textual. The texture of the textual is semiotic and syntactical. This means that the generation of a text is a displacement of immediate presence into the semantic field. Language can never get beneath itself, because its speech acts are always a further semantic displacement. Even if theology speaks softly and remains hidden behind cloistered walls, its speech is a public process using a public code and a public dictionary. Neologistic flourishes make sense or have meaning because of their connections in the semantic field. Theological language and the theological use of language are augmentations within a semantics of meaning. Immediate events are deepened into experiential meaning through a displacement. Theology can be thought of as an experience, but it is an experience of itself internal to language. The substance of theological experience is the text. It is an experience in language.

Theology is delimited by the range of the semantic world. Its achievement is the deferral of immediate awareness into the controlled world of the text. The deferral makes a difference. The primary event is no longer itself. The body of the event has been exchanged for the subtle body of the text. A mask has been substituted for a face and can be assigned its role in the public theater of words. The actuality of speech initiates a public drama, and if we are going to position the practice of theology it will have to be here.

Theology cannot fall back on silence and claim a nonsemantic meaning for itself or claim that its display of meaning is nonsemantic. It has to live with its own creation. "Once speech has spoken, its voice establishes a world or a field, and that field is indissoluble, it cannot simply disappear or pass away.... While speech can be remembered it can never be re-called, it can never cease to be speech, never cease to be itself."[2] Theology cannot cease to be itself. It has its place in a domain of discourse that is on the deepest level indissoluble and public.

The positioning of the theological text in a public drama also means that the theologian has a public, and that part of understanding the process of theological thinking involves an acknowledgment of the social reality of the theologian. David Tracy has suggested that the theologian address three distinct publics: the wider society, the academy, and the church.[3] What we do when we are thinking theologically involves one or all of these publics as a reference group. Theology is as much implicated in the hearing and reading of these publics as in the speaking and writing of the theologian. Positioning the practice of theology is a public determination that does not always correspond to the private intention of the theologian. When we want to know what type of phenomenon is theological thinking, we will need to know where it is located in the dominant discursive patterns of its public reference group.

Starkly characteristic of much theological thinking is that it is a marginal process broken off from the regular norm-governed social relations of the three publics Tracy has identified as theological reference groups. The contemporary moment in the social history of theology is the story of a nomad filching ideas from neighboring disciplines to sustain its discourse or masquerading as a science in a pretense of acceptable normality.

Theologies of liberation draw their sustenance from the Marxist vision, with a nod toward religious experience. Process theologies translate traditional theological concepts into a Whiteheadian philosophical frame. The present argument clearly trades in the capital of deconstructionist philosophy.

Theology has become a hybrid discipline of theology and some other social science or philosophy. What is telling is that the conflict of interpretations is almost always a conflict between the imported and allied ideas, systems, or sciences, not an explicitly theological argument. One could drop theology from these hybrid inquiries without losing explanatory power.

This story with its characteristics of social drama is described by Victor Turner as a liminal period of cultural transformation.[4] Turner's analysis of social drama does not tell us why theological thinking has experienced a breach with its publics, but it tells us a lot about what it means to be thinking in the margins. Even in these margins, theological thinking is a symbolic process. Turner's comparative symbology provides a framework for seeing theological thinking as a representative symbolic process in comparison with other sets of symbolic processes.

The four phases in a social drama Turner says are accessible to observation are a breach of normal relations, mounting crisis, adjustive and redressive actions, and the reintegration with the group or legitimation of a separation from the group.[5] The time of the social drama between the breach and reintegration or legitimization has liminal characteristics. It is a time betwixt and between. A gap has appeared, a space of indetermination. Possibilities can be displayed; new arrangements formed; a new order established. The liminal forms of symbolic action that follow the breach subject all previous standards of order to criticism.[6] The redressive actions reflect the mounting crisis and sometimes contribute to it so that the phases are observable but not clearly distinct. It is also possible the liminal characteristics of the time following the breach mark the beginning of a marginal identity, unless the process is contained within the structure and counterstructure of a stable society.

Unless we are looking back on a liminal period that has come to a close, the outcome remains unprejudiced. That is, liminality is so characterized that its outcome is uncertain. The identifiable charac-teristics fashion an undetermined future. "Syntax and logic are *problematic* and not *axiomatic* features of liminality.... And if we find them we have to consider well their relation to activities that have as yet no structure, no logic, only potentialities for them."[7] Liminality designates an experimental field where not only new ideas or images appear but also new combinatory rules govern their dissemination.[8] The meaning of meaning has a fluctuating signification. Disciplines of meaning such as theology would float without anchor during liminal periods. This is a recognizable characteristic of liminality that can help us locate the practice of theological thinking.

The internal witness of theologians indicates that theology has experienced a breach with its publics, is in a state of crisis, and is a floating or nomad discipline. It appears to be in the liminal phase of a social drama. Its breach with its publics was the threshold of crisis that led to its present indetermination and possibilities for new self-understanding.

In a concluding section on the social reality of the theologian, Tracy has said:

> Each theologian has, in fact, internalized to various degrees three publics, not one. Each has experienced the force of conflicting interpretations and conflicting plausibility structures in any attempt to make sense of

reality. Most have experienced the evaporation and eventual collapse of any first naiveté toward that same reality. Many have come to recognize the presence of real doubt in authentic contemporary faith.[9]

The loss of the first naiveté requires a break with the norm-governed rules of ordinary discourse in theology's three publics. It is not excessively reductionistic to suggest in the marketplace of the wider public, in the groves of the academy, or behind the walls of the church that ordinary discourse and the natural attitude toward the world are literal and hence one-dimensional. To be clear and distinct and to mean what we say is to say one thing at a time with a direct reference to the world. Parsimony is usually valued in ordinary uses of language. Even when complexity is acknowledged, ambivalence and ambiguity are distrusted. Little evidence suggests the "common sense" of theology's three publics barters with anything other than Enlightenment coinage.

Theology is not at home with its modern publics. It has designated itself as living in a postcritical and postmodern time. Its second naiveté, toward the symbolism of the sacred, is an interpretive construction in the margins of ordinary discourse. Paul Ricoeur says that we "aim at a second naiveté in and through criticism. In short, it is by *interpreting* that we can *hear* again."[10] An interpretive text is substituted for an original text, and the rules governing this substitution constitute what has been called the hermeneutical field. These are not the rules of ordinary discourse. In fact they often suspend ordinary discourse by insertion of an *epoche* bracketing questions that concern correspondence with the world of reference, while allowing for the multiplication and deployment of meanings. Meanings multiply outside the limits of the secular city and outside the reach of ordinary discourse. The achievement of theology can be identified with its irrelevance in ordinary discourse.

Langdon Gilkey, in a footnote comment on German hermeneutical theology, compares it with a *Festung* or castle belonging to a reigning bishop that is removed high above a town at a time when the castle's presence is essentially unrelated to life in town except as a tourist curiosity. He asks:

> How can theological reflection, if it can, move intelligibly, honestly, and with regularity from our life in the town to an existence, insofar as such is possible, on these heights, and how does the Word of God heard there have credibility and usability in the life of the town?[11]

Gilkey warns against a tourist theology, but it may be that his image of a *Festung* coheres with the liminal characteristics of theological thinking, and instead of moving back into the town we will have to ask how liminal thinking can be credible and usable in its life. If theology is a liminal phenomenon, we misunderstand its potential if we try to relocate it to the center of societal life. Its relevance will have to be a feature of its liminality. It will only have an illusory relevance if it claims to be something other than what it is.

The breach between theology and its publics was and is a crisis of meaning. Gilkey correctly noted in 1969 that to question the meaning of a metaphysical-theological system is more radical than to question its validity.[12] When theological statements are no longer admitted as meaningful in ordinary discourse, then the whole discipline is displaced. When even theologians doubt the possibility of their work constituting explanatory or assertive conceptual systems, then they are either doing something else when they speak and write or they are doing nothing of significance. The concept of meaninglessness implies a total disjunction with what we understand to be the world as we ordinarily know it.[13]

The breach between theological thinking and the cultural mainstream appears to be caused by the emergent dominance of a secular spirit in culture. Theology appears to be a victim of secularization. Even if the church represents a community of cognitive deviance when compared with the academy or wider public, its deviance follows the rules of ordinary discourse. It sometimes describes a world-picture that is not meaningless but rather false from the perspective of a secular society. The church appears not to understand its discourse as work in a hermeneutical field. Symbolic meaning often decorates the periphery of secular culture but is not an enigma at its center.

If we are to position theological thinking we simply have to acknowledge that a literal reading of sacred symbol systems conflicts with the dominant secular spirit. This spirit, mood, or tone has accompanied the growth of our scientific-technological culture and is part of its legacy. Gilkey describes four characteristics of the secular spirit in a summary expression that is as important now as when he formulated it: Intelligibility is bounded by a sense of contingency, relativity, transience, and autonomy.[14] There is no warrant for an absolute, fixed, eternal, theonomous world view that is acceptable for secular understanding. "The given just appears; it can be described as it appears, and *that* is all that can be said."[15] If theology accepts as its task the description of the world within these limits, it is hard to determine how it can remain theology.

The redressive actions by many theologians to stay within the boundaries of ordinary discourse sometimes have made theology all but in title indistinguishable from history, philosophy, psychology, sociology, anthropology, political theory, literary criticism, and even some physical sciences. It is curious why theologians who work in an adjacent discipline such as sociology don't refer to their work as sociology and take their place with the sociologists or in the community of whatever discipline they have adopted. If theology belongs in the margins of secular culture it will have to shape and understand itself as a marginal discipline or else cease being theology.

If we do not construe theology to be a substitute discipline, we can assert that it is in a liminal state and that it is public discourse. This means it can become a mode of public liminality if theologians learn to live with the tension of being in the margins of the dominant secular culture. Theology then belongs to the counterstructure of its three publics, and it is in that counterstructure that we can position the practice of theological thinking.

The move to marginal status is pragmatic since theology itself cannot remain under the rules that govern secular discourse. This flight from the center gives us some idea of what theology is not, but we do not yet have an understanding of what theological thinking is. What we do know is that theological discourse cannot be the same as secular discourse. The concept of a second naiveté corresponds with an altered function of theological reflection that is also an elaboration of the meaning of the second naiveté.

The breach or wound in theological thinking is much deeper than its separation from its publics and justifies the separation from the dominant patterns of secular discourse. This breach is within the process of theological thinking and is also manifested in its content. Perhaps theology had to be pushed into a marginal identity before it could seriously take account of its internal wounds and implicit liminality.

As we have already suggested, the critical breach in theological thinking was the shattering of language as the mirror image of nature.[16] It had become increasingly clear that naming the animals removed them from nature and relocated them in a semantic world. Even more important is the recognition that the named animals are not animals but words governed not by natural forces but by the laws of syntax and lexical history. Naming substitutes words for things and forces, and although it may be our only access to meaning it is at the same time a breach with the phenomenality of things.

The seminal work of Michel Foucault, *The Order of Things,* shows that the disfranchisement of the mirror-metaphor is not an intellectual quirk but instead the expression of a major shift in thinking that is no less pervasive than the emergence of the classical thinking of the Enlightenment.

> The threshold between Classicism and modernity (though the terms themselves have no importance—let us say between our prehistory and what is still contemporary) had been definitely crossed when words ceased to intersect with representations and to provide a spontaneous grid for the knowledge of things.[17]

It is the relationship between words and things that has been fundamentally altered. The relationship between words and things introduces the problems of representation and reference. When language is reflexively folded back on itself to account for its own nature, it discovers itself, not nature, mirrored in the virtual space of its construction. Mirroring requires the presence of a material image to be reflected, and the only materiality present in the semantic field is the materiality of the speech act. Language can endlessly repeat and replicate itself. This can tighten its weave, giving the illusion of a continuous surface, and prompt a literalism that sees no blemish or wound to bring us back to the scene of origination. The continuous surface of a tight weave can easily let us forget that speech acts are a semantic cloth that covers or masks the whole of reality in the creation of meaning.

The scene of the origination of thinking is the scene of a wound. The wound is a gap in thinking containing what is unthought and must remain unthought. We acknowledge the unthought not in itself but only in the transgression of what we can think. It is a shadow that does not come into speech except for the silences and broken figures that have become so characteristic in modern voices.

> Man has not been able to describe himself as a configuration in the *episteme* without thought at the same time discovering both in itself and outside itself, at its borders yet also in its very warp and woof, an element of darkness, an apparently inert density in which it is embedded, an unthought which it contains entirely, yet in which it is also caught.[18]

The unthought is, according to Foucault, a "shadow" cast by men and women as they emerge in the field of knowledge and a "blind stain" by which it is possible to know them.[19] "In any case, the unthought has accompanied man, mutely and uninterruptedly, since the nineteenth century."[20]

What is repressed in the scene of origination is the economy of things and forces as they are given in relationship to each other. It is this economy that remains unthought and must remain unthought, because thinking is a substitute and substitutive activity. Repression occurs through the process of representation. When we look at object language it is very easy to see that, written or spoken, it evokes an object through a substitute that is not the object. The word *tree* is not a tree, it does not materially resemble a tree, and its use is wholly governed by a code separate from the life of a tree. The semantic tree can become mythological, anthropomorphic, or divine. It can be locked in botanical rhetoric or transgress these boundaries in a fanciful zoology of the imagination. The repression of the economics of force through semantic substitution of a textual world is an erasure of the body in its environment. There is only a trace of the body in the body of text, because it is always "other" than the text.

What is present in the text points to what is absent, but not directly. It points to an absence by always turning on both itself and what is present. It is really not possible to make a reference outside the text except to acknowledge that the object reference is absent and other than the text, because what is deferred is no longer present so that what is present differs from what is deferred. Force comes to meaning through a substitution that tames and civilizes so that it is no longer itself. Primal forces become secondary forces. The vicissitudes of instinct become the vicissitudes of meaning.[21] The images of forces or things are overdetermined at their origin in linguistic and extra-linguistic realities, but the extralinguistic connection is rapidly effaced by the inability to replicate it in the semantic realm. The wound, the shadow, the gap, the breach, the erasure, and other figures of brokenness metaphorically speak of this inability to replicate extra-linguistic connections in the semantic realm. They augment the spread of language and contribute to the creation of meaning while at the same time referring to the discontinuities of force and meaning at the origin of speech and writing. By imaging the failure of things and forces to speak on their own terms, the wounds draw speech toward a failure on its own terms. There are impertinences in the flow of speech acts. The imperialism of speech is forced to halt before the image of its origination.

Speech acts are forced into the recognition that they cannot exist prior to themselves. Understanding is not a standing under experience or a standing behind experience. It is a supplement.

The meaning of the message is not the meaning of experience, nor is it the meaning experience would have, prior to all expression if this were possible. It is the meaning that experience can *receive* in a discourse which articulates it according to a certain code.[22]

The theme is familiar. Life, forces, things come to meaning by becoming other than themselves. The supplement is not the code but the world articulated according to a code. Meaning is not the code. Meaning is the supplement.

The body of force has a dialectical relationship with its textual supplement, of which metaphoricity and metaphor are the textual representations. The overdetermination of meaning is a representational approximation of the overdetermination that is the origin of meaning. Meaning is created as the world is received into speech, but neither the world nor the rules of speech can by themselves account for the supplement. Meaning can replicate and repeat itself but not be its own origination. The dialectic of presence and absence that involves substitution and repression is the ever-present stain of the world on the world of meaning. This means that theological discourse supplements the world, is marked by a relationship to the world that remains fundamentally unthought, and can only know itself as a world of supplemental meanings.

This is not nearly as complex as it first appears. What is present in knowing is the substitute materiality of speech acts and what is absent are the primary relationships that constitute our embodiment in the world. The presence of the world is made meaningful and known through substitution. The presence is metaphorical. The literal presence of the world is absent in the semantic supplement and relates to its metaphorical presence as a dialectical other. The surplus of meaning in a metaphorical presence, metaphorical potential, is not more meaning but the reality that is other than meaning. The verticality of language resides in what it is not, and this is why any discursive discipline that in principle cannot delimit the range of its questions transgresses established meanings.

Theology cannot delimit the range of its questions. The simple entertainment of concepts of God, absolute reality, ultimate reality, supreme nothingness, or any other variation of "that than which nothing greater can be conceived," enfranchises an unrestricted range of questions. The surface of every text can be called into question and folded back on itself. Theology cannot be itself without discovering a material presence that embodies the absence of the otherness that is repressed. When Robert Scharlemann writes about "the being of God when God is not being God" he sees that "the word *God* refers to the word *word,* and the word *word* refers to the word *God* " in such a way that "God means the negative that can be instantiated upon any object and any subject by the saying of the word."[23] The word *God* transgressed the text not simply by being absent but by negating the text. Unless theological thinking prescinds from the exigencies of its own conceptuality it must entertain language in an extreme distention of intelligibility that makes it marginal to ordinary discourse.

The theological text imposes a sense of loss. This has sometimes been conceptualized as the death of God, and it is here that we see a direct relationship between theology and deconstruction. Carl Raschke's announcement of the end of theology combined with his thesis that "deconstruction is the death of God put into writing" is an exemplary agenda item for theological thinking that is self-consciously a liminoid genre.[24] Parable and apocalypse in Thomas Altizer and John Dominic Crossan trope the narrative flow in story-theologies, giving them vertical significance and adding to the agenda of theology as a liminoid genre.[25] The agenda is as complex as the texts to be victimized.

When theological thinking moves into the margins of ordinary discourse, the trajectory of its work is inverted. This is why the language of deconstruction rather than reconstruction seems closer to the actual practice of a postcritical theology. Since the work of theology is discursive, its shape is determined by our understanding of language.

> Where, at the end of the eighteenth century, it was a matter of fixing the frontiers of knowledge, it will now be one of seeking to destroy syntax, to shatter tyrannical modes of speech, to turn words around in order to perceive all that is being said through them and despite them.[26]

Here Foucault is not describing a deconstructionist hermeneutic that has a clear place in theology or philosophy. He is staying with the task inflicted on modern consciousness by Nietzsche, Marx, and Freud. They helped bring us to a knowledge of the wound that is part of knowledge. We now have had enough time to know that the wound doesn't heal: it is actually a part of what it means to think theologically.

Sublation and subversion mix as we shift the metaphor of theological

practice from transcendence to transgression. That is, the metaphor
of transgression is closer to the practice of theological thinking.

Transgression, of course, is not simply the act of passing over. It is a
movement-beyond which violates, penetrates, fractures. . . . Transgression
inscribes the *via rupta.* Interpretation is a *hostile* act in which interpreter
victimizes text. The followers of Hermes are, after all, thieves (who come
in the night?).[27]

The standard postcritical understanding of theological thinking as
the making of meaning needs a twist if we are also to understand its
transgressive character. As we have already noted, the making of
meaning is the substitution of signs (words), their dissemination, and
their display in multiple configurations. But the substitution is overdetermined: the dissemination and display is a dialectical performance
overspilling the semantic achievement even when it remains unthought. What is repressed, the body in the body of experience, can
always return through the seams and fissures in the body of the text
when the text is deconstructively displayed. The creation of meaning
can be transformed into a dialectical theater by drawing the semantic
achievement into the margins of discourse where the seams are more
clearly displayed. The tone is depressive because the deconstructionist
display pulls theological thinking toward what was repressed by the
very fact of representational origination in metaphorical substitution.
The dialectical theater approximates a reenactment of the scene of
origination. The dialectical theater in theological deconstruction is a
theater of memory that returns meaning to the scene of its origination
without ever being able to go behind it. The dialectical theater is a
theater of acknowledgment that the vital forces transformed by a
work into meaning remain intact. Meaning is transgressed in order to
be known as meaning. Theological construction brings force to
meaning through substitution and repression; theological deconstruction brings meaning to force by displaying the negative capability of
speech acts in the witness to their origination. Thinking can turn
language back on itself through speech and writing in a witness to
the metaphoricity of meaning. This act is an acknowledgment of force
and meaning. It is creation and memory.

The practice of theological thinking as deconstruction is a choice
to subvert quotidian patterns of discourse to display better the
supplementarity of the text that is its own achievement. It is a choice
to define a space where language can be drawn into a free performance
displaying its own material presence and witness to an otherness that

is absent. It is a process or practice that has shaped itself, defined its task, and relates to its publics as a liminoid phenomena. The breach that theological thinking has experienced with its publics is not merely a matter of modern circumstance. Deconstruction in theology in fact causes a breach with the discourses of its publics and a breach within itself in order to be what it is. Like other liminoid genres, it can only "develop apart from the central economic and political processes, along the margins, in the interfaces and interstices of central and servicing institutions."[28] Its own alienation from the center of discourse subverts the alienation from the experience of vitalizing forces that define that center. This is part of the significance of theology as a liminoid genre. Marginality imparts the freedom for a play of words and images replete with possibilities for new configurations, exploratory fissures, and movements toward and among fields of force.

Theological thinking is relevant because it is other than ordinary discourse and is itself a discourse that can display the otherness of its semantic achievement. It is needed by its three publics as a form of public liminality, as a public critique, and as a display of alternative possibilities. Its internal breach relieves its publics from a tight weave of meanings blind to their metaphorical potential. Theology with its radical conceptuality can create spaces in ordinary thinking and rend the fabric of ordinary discourse. This is a process and practice that offers freedom and space for new meanings and a memory of the significance of meaning.

Victor Turner suggests that:

> In the evolution of man's symbolic "cultural" action, we must seek those processes which correspond to openendedness in biological evolution. I think we have found them in those liminal, or "liminoid" (post-industrial revolution), forms of symbolic action, those genres of free-time activity, in which all previous standards and models are subjected to criticism, and fresh new ways of describing and interpreting sociocultural experience are formulated.[29]

The danger is that what is liminal becomes stabilized and what is marginal becomes central. Theology needs to stay on the margins to be itself. Its relevance for its publics is the open-endedness of its presence.

NOTES

1. Kenneth Burke, *The Rhetoric of Religion: Studies in Logology* (Berkeley and Los Angeles: Univ. of California Press, 1970), vi.

2. Thomas J. J. Altizer, *The Self-Embodiment of God* (New York: Harper & Row, 1977), 16.

3. David Tracy, *The Analogical Imagination: Christian Theology and the Culture of Pluralism* (New York: Crossroad, 1981), 5.

4. Victor Turner, *Dramas, Fields and Metaphors: Symbolic Action in Human Society* (Ithaca, N.Y.: Cornell Univ. Press, 1974), 37–42.

5. Ibid., 38–41.

6. Ibid., 15.

7. Ibid., 255.

8. Victor Turner, *Process, Performance and Pilgrimage* (New Delhi, India: Concept Publishing Co., 1979), 21.

9. Tracy, *Analogical Imagination*, 30.

10. Paul Ricoeur, *The Symbolism of Evil* (New York: Harper & Row, 1967), 351.

11. Langdon Gilkey, *Naming the Whirlwind: The Renewal of God-Language* (Indianapolis: Bobbs-Merrill, 1969), 199–200.

12. Ibid., 17.

13. Ibid., 19.

14. Ibid., 39–71.

15. Ibid., 41.

16. Cf. Richard Rorty, *Philosophy and the Mirror of Nature* (Princeton: Princeton Univ. Press, 1979).

17. Michel Foucault, *The Order of Things: An Archaeology of the Human Sciences* (New York: Vintage Books, 1973), 304.

18. Ibid., 326.

19. Ibid., 322–26.

20. Ibid., 327.

21. Paul Ricoeur, *Freud and Philosophy: An Essay on Interpretation* (New Haven: Yale Univ. Press, 1970), 6.

22. Vincent Descombes, *Modern French Philosophy* (Cambridge: Cambridge Univ. Press, 1980), 98.

23. Robert P. Scharlemann, "The Being of God When God Is Not Being God," in *Deconstruction and Theology* (New York: Crossroad, 1982), 102.

24. Carl A. Raschke, "The Deconstruction of God," in *Deconstruction and Theology*, 27.

25. Cf. Thomas J. J. Altizer, *The Self-Embodiment of God* (New York: Harper & Row, 1977); *Total Presence* (New York: Seabury Press, 1980); and John Dominic Crossan, *The Raid on the Articulate: Eschatology in Jesus and Borges* (New York: Harper & Row, 1976); *The Dark Interval* (Niles, Ill.: Argus Communications, 1975).

26. Foucault, *Order of Things*, 298.

27. Mark C. Taylor, "Text as Victim," in *Deconstruction and Theology*, 65.

28. Turner, *Process, Performance and Pilgrimage*, 53.

29. Turner, *Dramas, Fields and Metaphors*, 15.

Desire and the Subtle Body
of Theology

For the wanderer brings down from the mountainside not a handful of
earth to the valley, all indescribable but the word he has gained there,
pure, the yellow and blue gentian. Are we perhaps here only to say:
house, bridge, brook, gate, jug, olive tree, window—at best: pillar, tower
... but to *say* them, understand me, *so* to say them as the things within
themselves never thought to be.
—Rainer Maria Rilke, "The Ninth Elegy," *The Duino Elegies*

The conceptual aim of theology differs from the aim of the study
of religion as it seeks to say things that the things within themselves
never thought to be. The cultural and experiential field, the language
and methodological structures may be similar, and the participants
may be the same. But thinking and speaking theologically are distinguishable from empirical studies, philological investigations, and
historical reflections when examined in a theory of discourse. There
are theological moments in general scholarship that can sometimes
confuse the issue, but this occurs only when the rules of discourse
are modulated to access a theological intention. It is this intention
that needs to be investigated in a critical theory of discourse before
we can fully characterize the practice of theological thinking, describe
its nature, and assess its importance for a postcritical and postmodern
culture. Theology is thought in the margins of scholarship because it
can no longer be itself and simply pretend to describe the world as
it is or articulate religious doctrines that purport to describe the
world as it is.

It is the consonance with general cultural forms that enfranchised
the medieval school theologians' notion of theology as *habitus,* a
cognitive disposition and orientation of the soul, or the breakup of

theologia into disciplines in the encyclopedic movement of the German *Aufklärung* and the more recent pedagogical separation of theology into functional specialties.[1] It is a further shift in general cultural forms, one Michel Foucault has likened to a geological plate shift that motivates new inquiry into the possibility and place of theological thinking.

The critical breach in postmodern thinking shifted the ground so that historiographical realisms dissolved in ironic solutions that altered the meanings of universal histories or personal narratives. The discoveries by Nietzsche, Freud, and Marx of disguise, distortion, condensation, displacement, and ideology in the primal representations of language that we have described cleared the ground for theories of discourse that would have been too radical if the wound had not already been inflicted across the display of history and culture. The fantasy of literalism was further eroded by philosophies of distortion, ambivalence, and ambiguity, and language was turned on itself as both the mode and object of inquiry.

Ferdinand de Saussure discovered that "terminological difficulties in linguistics resulted from the fact that these terms tried to *name* substances or objects (the 'word,' the 'sentence') while linguistics was a science characterized by the absence of such substances."[2] This discovery had implications for critical theory in all disciplines that had to do with words and discourse.

The scene of origination is not simply a nominal substitution. Meaning is made determinate through the elaboration of a system of difference. In language, identity is not the congruent overlay of a signifier on itself; identity is the establishment or perception of a difference.[3] It is the internal negation of other elements in the system, a difference that fixes an identity. It is the system of internal differentiation and not mirroring that creates representational meaning. The creation of meaning is the deferral of immediate awareness into the controlled world of the text. There is no simple correspondence that is an identity because identity in the manifest content of meaning is a negation and a difference. Identity in difference is the metaphorical basis of meaning, the poetic basis of mind.

Pragmatic competencies are needed for the work of most discursive disciplines. A choice is made to delimit the rules of representation so that there are boundaries of intelligibility that usually coincide with the scope of the discipline. In the ordinary uses of language these rules are conventions that are seldom noticed except by the linguist.

In technical disciplines the rules are often quite explicit, so that you readily know when you are working inside or outside the discipline. The data field of meaningful experience is itself prefigured by the rules of representation. What is hidden behind language usage lies fallow in the shadow of the scene of origination.

The residue of what remains unsaid is a problem only if significant gaps appear that challenge the explanatory power of the governing paradigm or if the discipline is internally unrestrictive in the scope of its questioning. The history of disciplines is usually marked by a narrowing focus of attention so that to forget what is unsaid is an expected correlate of an increasingly refined achievement. Bringing to expression what is unsaid in one discipline is relegated to the responsibilities of another. If something important is left unsaid, it is surely thought to be someone else's task to say it. It is only when a discipline is internally unrestrictive that the unsaid presses for a saying. The establishment of identity through the determination of differences is no longer a pragmatic solution but is now the problem that makes every achievement incomplete. The expansion of inquiry enlarges the residue of what is unsaid. The expansion of meaning is a semantic extension of the surface of the text that can never get behind itself without ceasing to be a text. Intertextual referencing is a variation of textual extension. There is still no text but the present text.

We usually prescind from the problem by narrowing the scope of inquiry to serve specified intellectual or practical goals. Thinking can augment the intelligibility of experience without ever turning on itself and the scene of its own origination. It is only when we think about thinking and its material expression in language convolutes that pragmatic solutions are not feasible. We cannot delimit the rules of representation when seeking to represent representation. Of course this would not appear to be pertinent to thinking unless the use of language was faltering as a representational scheme. This usually only occurs when we are thinking "in extremis" at the borders of intelligibility.

It is, for example, in poetic, metaphysical, theological, and even psychotic discourses that we regularly approach these boundaries. A combination of factors takes discourse to the extreme boundaries of intelligibility, particularly the inability internally to restrict the scope of questioning. Theology is of particular interest for a critical theory of discourse and what appears to be an epistemology of darkness, because it traditionally does not restrict the scope of its questioning; its use of language has faltered as a representational scheme, and yet it persists. In some ways it is more interesting to explore than the Western metaphysical tradition because of its greater unwillingness or incapacity to bury what appear to be dead terms and concepts. It continually resurrects, resuscitates, and often disguises words and ideas in new semantic displays of meaning. It seldom mistakes its work for a literal description of the world of things and experience without qualifications and meta-analyses. Theology is one of the most consistent and self-conscious examples of representational discourse without an external reference.

What are we doing when we think theologically? Theological thinking's persistence, its unrestrictive scope, and its faltering representational schemes combine to characterize a discursive activity that cannot viably be thought of as a descriptive science. The disproportion between the demands of an unrestricted desire to know and the inability to ascertain the descriptive relevance of theological representational schemes suggests theological thinking is responding to the demand in a way not coincidental with traditional cognitive claims. The problem arises because what appears to be a descriptive use of language is not. Doctrines of analogy and theories of symbolism or metaphorical-language usage all acknowledge the gap between force and the body of language, and in theology the acknowledgment is extended to the gap between the immanent transcendence of an unrestricted desire to know and the signified transcendental that is wholly other from theology's representational schemes.[4] When theology talks about God, the Brahman, ultimate reality, or Holy Nothingness instead of talking about talking about God, the exigencies of the unrestricted desire to know force the question of the gap between immediate experience and meaning into awareness. *Theology's god is always a god of the gaps.*

The problem of crossing the gap between the mediacy of meaning into the complex of the body in the general economy of forces is that the negation will have to be all-inclusive. That is, the representational scheme will have to be negated, and that will leave no context in which one can mark a difference. We will have to stay within meaning, only approximately characterizing the general economy of forces through concepts of otherness, and draw near the gap through figures of brokenness. These are two different works even when they overlay temporally. Conceptualization is a mediation of meaning. It is a substitutionary activity that creates a supplementary text. Force is brought to meaning in absentia. The substance of the experience is now the materiality of the text. On the other hand, drawing near the gap, bringing meaning to force, is what we do with the text, but always within the supplementarity of the text. We can work the text to bring it close to the general economy of forces, but this work will remain differentiated within the semantics of meaning. When meaning is brought to force its internal weave of intelligibility is loosened so that it stands with a fresh permeability amidst the economy of forces. Force will continue to be brought to meaning, but in new configurations.

This second movement is dialectical and has an antiphenomenological bias. It lifts the Husserlian epoché protecting constructions of meaning construed as essences. What lies behind this second movement is the acknowledgment that desire lacks fullness or completeness of expression in a representational scheme. What is lacking is the presence of the complex of forces that is represented. There is a primary experience, but it is the experience of the present materiality of the text. When the text gaps there is an immediate experience of a lack that gives justification to the assumption of an extralinguistic body of experience.

The problem we are describing is not unlike Freud's attempts to characterize the unconscious. He asks, "How are we to arrive at a knowledge of the unconscious? It is of course only as something conscious that we know it, after it has undergone transformation or translation into something conscious."[5] He then goes on to say that we know the unconscious through the gaps in consciousness. Consciousness is always faltering before the ideal of complete intelligibility. The gaps in consciousness presuppose what is not conscious. Freud's specific description of an unconscious system is an analysis and reflection of consciousness. The concept of the unconscious is a trope in the conscious display of meaning that brings us to a memory of the forgetfulness of the energy of the psyche. The concept of the unconscious semantically embodies the absence of forces in the display of meaning so that meaning is conditioned by the otherness of desire. Consciousness has reason to be suspicious of itself. It must refuse language its self-containment without confusing its own references to immediate experience with literal representation.

To proceed, psychoanalysis had to develop a genre of rhetoric that worked in duplicities. What was in a semantics of meaning had to double for what was in the economics of force without the fixity of meaning denying the motility of force. What appeared was a fictive elaboration of the medical empiricism associated with case histories.[6] The family constellation was augmented by an Oedipal drama with mythological roots in a primal scene in the prehistory of culture. Individual stories were sublated into a drama of Eros, Thanatos, and Ananke.

Freud's psychoanalytic studies are a model in the rhetoric of poesis. The figure of the unconscious was elaborated through functional and topographical hypotheses and particularly through the concept of psychosexuality so that he could implicate the full range of narrative meaning in the force of desire. The hidden god of sexuality continually drew Freud's discourse toward the boundary of the gap between force and meaning. The sensual, desiring physical body was given such prominence in the subtle body of the text that when conscious thinking would become rigorous and try to tighten the weave of its own explanations it would convolute on its own principle of explanation and disclose the gap at the scene of its origination.

The psychoanalytic transgression of the text from within is an important movement for us to keep in mind when we turn back to the question of what it means to think theologically. We could almost stop here if our only problem were to articulate a competency for subverting the claim to semantic completeness and if we had but one god, the *deus absconditus* of infantile psychosexuality, in the texts of religious traditions. The problem with Freud's solution is that it is not complex enough (1) to subvert a far-reaching textual tradition that is not fully personal and (2) to satisfy the demands of a discipline that is internally unrestrictive in the scope of its questioning. Even if we conceive of an unrestricted desire to know as a sublimation of psychosexuality, its figuration is now complex enough to constitute an erotic bonding with a world of meanings that exceeds personal narratives. Theology, without denying psychoanalytic psychosexuality, has elaborated the meaning of desire and thereby implicated the whole world of specific meanings in the psychoanalytic problem of the unconscious.

Psychosexuality is itself a textual representation that elaborates the meaning of the unconscious. It is a development of the subtle body of the text and not an immediate experience of the body. The exigencies of theological thinking remove the restrictions from the meaning of desire, which is no more than another textual elaboration of the otherness at the origins of meaning. It is the simplicity of the retorsive device of not without contradiction being able to question the possibility of questioning that enfranchises the internally unrestrictive scope of questioning. Everything is questionable. This claim marks an exigency in thinking and is not an expectation that theology would ever approximate knowing the complete set of answers to the complete set of questions. The unrestricted desire to know is part of what is semantically given in explicating a theory of theological discourse. It is a characteristic of theological text production.

What is also given is a textual tradition, including the literature of a sacred canon. In practice, theological thinking usually begins by thinking about this literary legacy. Scripture and tradition are obvious content for theological reflection. It is only because the representational scheme of most traditional theological literature has lost its descriptive credibility that we have been asking what it means to be thinking theologically. If theologians could have referenced coherently the theological tradition in the intertextual schemes of contemporary thinking without leaving heaps of linguistic debris, they probably would have remained unaware of the breach between the complex body of forces and the body of language. But since this postcritical hiatus cannot be ascribed to an aberration of modern consciousness, theology has had to defamiliarize itself retrospectively with the cognitive and descriptive claims of its inherited tradition. We would have to become forgetful of our forgetfulness at the origin of meaning simply to maintain a "monumental history" of great moments of revelation. This would be the aberration in consciousness.

What Ray Hart calls the "fundament" in the immediate body of religious experience is absent in the literary legacy of theology. What is present points to this absence. "Tradition and scripture are *there,* but revelation as fundament, while there in them, is not *there* in them in the way that they are there: that is the core of this area of problematic."[8] First-order theological thinking, the inverbalization of an event or events, has always been the repression of the immediate body of forces, the deferral of desire into imaginative expression. As Gordon Kaufman has suggested in his description of second-order theology, the recognition that all first-order theology is an imaginative construction (second-order theology) leaves us with a task of the third order.[9] What do we do after we have gone through the work of relinquishing theology from the task of literal description and recognize that that was never its actual achievement? Even historical theology could hardly be content with the repetition and recital of past theological formulations without at the same time reflecting on the character of the representational schemes in which they reside. Systematic and philosophical theology will have to take direct responsibility for fashioning a task that is incorrigibly imaginative.

First-order theology begins metaphorically and dialectically. This is what is recognized in second-order critical theory. The scene of origination is a passage, a repression, and a deferral of desire. The trajectory of substitution is the bringing of the forces of immediate experience to meaning. The linkage of dissimilar realms in the imaginative act is the primary experience of metaphoricity. The relationship of the dissimilar realms is dialectical. They always belong to each other, so that even when the semantic realm is a mediating substitution for the fundament of an earlier experience it is immediate in its own material presence. There is always the primary experience of the new text that can then be mediated in a yet newer text. The experience of the text can be represented in a new text and at the same time the old text implicated in intertextual references. The text is then overdetermined in realms of force and meaning, although it can only be known in its semantic display. This means theological construction can intentionally double itself in a semantic overdetermination as well as be dialectically overdetermined in the realms of force and meaning by the nature of its investment in language usage. Because of the natural dialectical relationship at the scene of origination, theology can also turn on its linguistic achievement and function deconstructively. It can breach its own semantic surface and draw meaning toward its repressed origins. Third-order theology oscillates between constructive and deconstructive possibilities. This oscillation impacts the characterization of either movement. The dialectic is enhanced by the complementarity of the two movements. In complementary modes, construction does not aim at seamless closure. Deconstruction does not bring any closure to the work at all.

The constructive work of theology is the production of a text. Either primary forces are lifted into the referential order of language or a prior text is interpretively transformed. The founding of meaning, which we have already described as a substitutionary and repressive action at the metaphorical basis of mind, is also an elaboration of the substitute representation. If there were simply a substitution of a word or image corresponding to a direct perception, theological discourse would approximate a descriptive science with a few basic qualifications. Instead the founding of meaning is an affair of complexity. Even the singular perception is known against a back-world of complexity that is the representational scheme.[10] The problem is that we cannot entertain a single word or image without schematization. Words are always referenced in relationship with other words. There can be both the elaboration of the word in the representational scheme and the elaboration of the representational scheme.

The inverbalization of an event places it in the holy history, against a resurrection narrative, in a legal list-literature or in the struggles of a polytheistic pantheon. Not only is the representation of the event rendered complex by textual references, but also this back-world can itself be expanded, folded, and referenced intertextually. Meanings are repeated and multiplied. The constructive work of theology is limited only by the imaginative capacities of theologians. There is no disciplinary limitation on the complexity of texts entertained in its reflections. The inverbalization of the event can be disseminated freely because theology cannot withhold meaningful connection after formulating concepts of "that than which nothing greater can be conceived," ultimate reality, the ground of Being or a wholly other Lord of the Worlds. This is a unique feature of the internally unrestrictive claim of theology. It has metaphysical expansiveness with immediate reference to the concrete inverbalization of an event.

Whole texts are subject to the same type of referential expansion. What is usually called hermeneutics is a pattern of intertextual referencing. The dialogical model of theological disciplines is the surface manifestation of intertextual referencing. If theological subdisciplines such as theology and literature or theology and the social sciences are not explicitly subordinationist, what we usually recognize is a hermeneutic of intertextual referencing. Otherwise we have simple expansion of theology, sociology, or literary-critical theory that remains unconscious of its implicit textual problems.

It is the problem of the text that too often remains unthought in theology. Regions of intelligibility can be interlaced and the patterns of reference can expand without the recognition that this is the work of the production of a text. As long as we think a text is mimetic of some real world, the purpose of text production is accurate description. But postcritical thinking understands text production to be semiosis. The text is built metaphorically. The commitment to accurate description is the metaphorizing of a reality principle. Text production can have other purposes. For example, if we want to bring the dialectical relationship between force and meaning to articulation so that it can be experienced directly in the text, the text will have to be highly overdetermined. Even values such as lucidity are overdetermined. We can be referring to seeing clear patterns in the text or seeing clearly through the text to the darkness of what is unthought and unknown. If we want to see through meaning into the darkness of the unthought in the body of experience, then the work of text production is a defamiliarization through the overdetermination of meaning. The descriptive credibility of the text is loosened.[11] The world is made strange.

Significance is here distinguished from meaning. Meaning is founded in the patterns of connectedness within the text or in intertextual referencing. Significance is the combining of meaning with importance in the fullness of the complete body of forces. It is referencing the extralinguistic connection at the origin of meaning and the ongoing dialectical relationship that constitutes the ontological root of metaphor. The theological figuration of meaning in ultimate terms reflexively embodies the internal unrestrictiveness to the scope of its questions, making it responsible to questions of significance as well as to questions of meaning.

When Roland Barthes asks, "What is significance?" he replies that "It is meaning, *insofar as it is sensually produced*."[12] The sensual production of the text is not description alone. The body of meaning has to be connected to the importance of the body of experience, which can be no less than the experience of our own bodies in their connectedness with the world. Text, body, and world intersect in the sensual imagination. Barthes also suggests that the most erotic portion of the body is where a garment gapes.[13] It is the "staging of appearance as disappearance," the flash or the trace that seduces. It is the text in its origination that imposes a state and a scene of loss. What appears disappears in the representational scheme. *Our relationship to loss is desire.* The theological question of significance is a reaching into the unthought darkness of desire.

To achieve significance, theology must rend the fabric of descriptive discourse and let the text momentarily gape in a flash of sensuality. A deconstructive theology continually recapitulates the scene of the origination of meaning. It implicates the world of constructive description in desire.

The significance of the text is only known as it is violated or transgressed. As Mark Taylor has suggested, the text must be a victim of interpretation.[14] We see a model for this victimization in the semiotics of poetry that Harold Bloom has been able to extend into a psychoanalytic framework implicating the fullness of the metaphor of our subjectivity.[15] Michael Riffaterre describes the process through a poetic tropology of indirection. He says that "maximal catachresis at the lexematic level of individual words or phrases coincides with significance at the textual level."[16] The broken figure is at the same time a figure of brokenness. The text dwells in the tension between meaning and significance. The yellow and blue gentian is at the same time the indescribable handful of earth that the wanderer first knew on the mountainside.

The practice of theology oscillates between the raid on the inarticulate and the raid on the articulate.[17] It is a dialectical theater of desire and meaning. Desire is the root of theological thinking. The dissemination of meaning is the necessary indirection of its fulfillment. The accession to theological language brings the fullness of world and experience onto the stage of the dialectical theater. There is an alternating rhythm between the sublation of the body of experience and the subversion of the body of the text.

Theology is significant only when it is a radical theology, only when it transgresses its own sense of transcendence. Maximal catachresis in theological thinking is the death of God, the end of history, the descent into hell and eternal death. The grand tropes fashioned by Altizer and other radical theologians are a commitment to the significance of theological thinking. They restore to theology the medieval notion of *habitus,* a disposition and orientation of the soul that denies life neither its meaning nor its significance.

NOTES

1. Edward Farley, *Theologia: The Fragmentation and Unity of Theology in Education* (Philadelphia: Fortress Press, 1983), 35, 63.

2. Fredric Jameson, *The Prison House of Language* (Princeton: Princeton Univ. Press, 1972), 13.

3. Ibid., 35.

4. Cf. Bernard Lonergan, *Insight: A Study of Human Understanding* (New York: Philosophical Library, 1957), chap. 19.

5. Sigmund Freud, *The Standard Edition of the Complete Psychological Works of Sigmund Freud,* 24 vols. (London: Hogarth Press and the Institute of Psychoanalysis, 1953–74), 14:166.

6. Cf. James Hillman, "The Fiction of a Case History: A Round," in *Religion as Story*, ed. James Wiggins (New York: Harper & Row, 1975), 126.

7. Emerich Coreth, *Metaphysics* (New York: Herder & Herder, 1968), 48.

8. Ray L. Hart, *Unfinished Man and the Imagination: Toward an Ontology and a Rhetoric of Revelation* (New York: Herder & Herder, 1968), 104.

9. Gordon D. Kaufman, *An Essay on Theological Method* (Missoula, Mont.: Scholars Press, 1979), 38.

10. Hart, *Unfinished Man,* 94.

11. Cf. Michael Riffaterre, *Semiotics of Poetry* (London: Methner & Co., 1978), 10.

12. Roland Barthes, *The Pleasure of the Text* (New York: Hill & Wang, 1975), 61.

13. Ibid., 9–10.

14. Mark Taylor, "Text as Victim," in *Deconstruction and Theology* (New York: Crossroad, 1982).

15. Cf. Harold Bloom, *The Anxiety of Influence: A Theory of Poetry* (New York: Oxford Univ. Press, 1973).

16. Riffaterre, *Semiotics of Poetry,* 80.

17. Cf. John Dominic Crossan, *The Raid on the Articulate: Comic Eschatology in Jesus and Borges* (New York: Harper & Row, 1976).

Appendix: The Deconstruction of the Theology of Proclamation

A postmodern theology is not defined by the object of its inquiry. It is a textual production in which the author is written into the work as a theologian by implicating the text in the exigencies of the unrestricted scope of theological inquiry. The postmodern theological text will be marked and sometimes re-marked by fissures wrought by limiting questions, poetic indirections, and figures of brokenness. Theology can be reread and rewritten with the benefit of these levers of textual intervention that do not allow an easy forgetfulness of the origin of theological thinking as a work of language and desire.

Thomas J. J. Altizer's understanding of the death of God is such a deconstructive lever of intervention, one that forces a new reading and writing of theology in its postmodern condition. Altizer is not clearly identified as a deconstructionist thinker, but a retrospective reading of his work can lead to primal thinking that restores to theology its vitality and draws the reader close to the scene of origination of fully theological thought.

I have appended this study of Altizer to the development of an epistemology of darkness because I think Altizer's books *Total Presence* and *The Self-Embodiment of God* combine to form one of the most important statements of what it means to think theologically in the closing time of this century. The radical theology in these two volumes has an original and mature voice. Unlike so many of his contemporaries, Altizer is not simply talking about the possibility of doing theology but is thinking and writing theologically.

Theologians who are only comfortable within familiar formulations of Christian doctrine will want to dismiss Altizer, because his work is a descent into the unfamiliar worlds of silence and darkness. However, it will not be easy to dismiss his work: the world into which he descends is, as the subtitle of *Total Presence* suggests, a world of the language of Jesus and the language of today.

The originality of Altizer's work is in part the originality of his work as a reader. In particular, his reading of literary and philosophical precursors, Blake, Hegel, and Nietzsche, who are themselves transgressors of the Western tradition, and the transgressive reading of his more immediate teachers, Joachim Wach, Mircea Eliade, and Paul Tillich, have made him the most important theological interpreter of the "blank spaces" that significantly inhabit the texts defining our Western theological tradition. His sensitivity to the dialectic between what is said and not said, between speech and silence, between presence and absence, situates his theological reflections at the root of what we call consciousness and celebrate as experience. Hence, his Christology is at the same time fundamental, historical, and systematic theology. The articulation of doctrine is a wrestling with history and epistemology in the recognition that what has been said was at one time not said and that it is in this difference that theology establishes its significance.

In his recent work it is clear that language and speech mark the theater of theological reflection. "Theology today is most fundamentally in quest of a language and mode whereby it can speak. . . . Speech is the most immediate and intimate arena of our life and identity."[1] Although this theme has its clearest expression in *The Self-Embodiment of God* and *Total Presence,* it resonates throughout all the earlier work. The resonance in his work is the sense of the dissonance between our life in the postmodern world and traditional theological categories.

The examples are plentiful.

Finally, all Eliade's theological difficulties derive from an inadequate theological language. He is forced to speak in the language of traditional theological conceptions although his own thought has taken him far beyond the province of the theological tradition.[2]

The greater part of the ambiguity and confusion in Kierkegaard's work derives from his desperate effort to speak in the language of theological orthodoxy.[3]

What is experienced as a failure or diminishment of meaning is transformed into a calling. "Only a theology unveiling a new form of the Word, a form that is present or dawning in the immediate and contemporary life of faith, can be judged to be uniquely and authentically Christian."[4]

It is a calling that is also a judgment. "As the historical world of Christendom sinks ever more deeply into the darkness of an irrevocable past, theology is faced with the choice either of relapsing into a dead and archaic language or of evolving a whole new form of speech."[5]

By the time he gets to the book on Blake it is clear that a new literary genre, for Blake the poetic apocalypse, was needed to speak theologically. The divided consciousness seen as the result of objective representation is viewed as a closure.

So long as consciousness remains bound to *Vorstellung*, it must exist in an alienated form, closed to the inner reality of itself by its very belief in an alien Other.[6]

There is a profound humanism to these insights that Altizer describes as a bitter truth. He acknowledges that language must be embodied in consciousness and experience if it is to have any meaning.

One of the bitterest truths which we have been forced to learn is that all language is human language, even including language about God, and human language, as opposed to a divine or angelic language, is empty and meaningless when it evokes no response, and thus ceases to be a language when it is no longer capable of being the instrument of communication or expression.[7]

This means that any epistemic privilege given to the traditional language of faith is unreal. Modern consciousness can no longer subordinate itself to a claim of a transcendent reality that in itself negates the intelligibility of modern consciousness. The *Descent into Hell* is

written with the conviction that Christianity has undergone a revolutionary transformation in the modern world, and the primary responsibility of the theologian is to come to understand the meaning of a new form of faith which is already manifest and real.[8]

This new form of faith must be a response to the immanence of God, which is the death of God. The message and mission of Jesus is not a prolepsis of the future. "Immanence is opposed to transcendence in the sense that immanence *is* that which transcendence *was*."[9] Altizer tenaciously holds to the cosmic significance of the incarnation without ever letting go of the claims of modern consciousness.

The key to understanding this double grasp is his understanding of language and its enactment in speech. We are immediately into the central issues of *The Self-Embodiment of God*. Altizer thinks of faith as the fullness of speech, and this is an important complexity in his thought that keeps his discussion of the fully incarnate Christ from being identified with a cosmic or historical literalism. "Faith begins as a response to the mystery of speech, or a response to the mystery of the primal ground of speech."[10] The mystery of speech is also the mystery of silence. Speech acts. "Speech is simultaneously both the origin of all meaning and identity and a fall from the quiescence and peace of silence."[11]

The fall that is the origin of meaning and identity is the actualization of a difference. It is the relationship of identity and difference that introduces negation into the seemingly innocent garden of original meaning. The serpent in our midst is metaphorical and is metaphor. Altizer has abjured metaphorical readings of theology, but in his understanding of identity and difference has affirmed an expanded meaning of the fundamental metaphoricity of all speech acts. The origin of identity is a displacement and a substitution. His enactment of speech is a deferring that is also a differing and closely resembles what Jacques Derrida has called *differance*. The origin of identity is the substitution of a signifier, a name, for the transcendental signified, and a displacement into a network of signifiers. This is not Altizer's language. His language focuses less on the structure and more on the act of speech.

"When identity is so called out of itself, thereby embodying call in act, it realizes a new identity of itself, and realizes that identity only by losing all identity which is not embodied in its act."[12] The identity that is embodied in the act differs from the act because the act becomes other than itself in its own realization.

> Speech realizes itself by transcending itself, but it transcends itself by actualizing itself in that hearing which is speech. Then speech speaks by hearing, and by hearing itself. But speech can hear itself only by being other than itself, even if in that otherness, it truly realizes itself as speech.[13]

The context of Altizer's epistemological development in this book is the questioning whether we can name God and actually speak that name. Uttering the name of God is both exodus and judgment. "God is the name of exile" is a cryptic formulation of the experience of this privileged speech act. The reason for this exile is the finite nature of consciousness and speech, the necessary dialectic between identity and difference. Identity is possible only in the embodiment of difference. "Only the presence of difference calls identity forth, and it calls it forth in its difference from itself, in its difference from an identity which is eternally the same."[14] The actualization of a name in speech is not the attachment of a label or simple augmentation. It is a transformation of experience into a different order or realm. When experience is structured like a language, we are simply having a different experience. Speech has a violence. It violates the order of silence not simply by intruding on the quiescence of silence but by embodying it as something other than itself. "It is its integral and intrinsic negation, a negation wherein an undifferentiated silence becomes the opposite of itself."[15] Speech embodies difference. It establishes an identity through difference from a simple identity, an identity which is only itself. Simple identity would have to remain mute, because it simply is what it is. The dilemma for those who yearn for a world of simple identities is that they can never name this world or God, because the naming creates a difference and the identity is other than itself. In this sense speech is the intelligible residue of forgetfulness. The trace of the forgotten is the presence of what is absent.

A deconstructionist hermeneutic is implied by Altizer's understanding of speech and is explicitly manifested in his transgressive reading of the tradition. "... the speech of speech must violate itself, and violate itself in its own embodiment."[16] Speech can never be fixed in the satisfaction of descriptive simple identities, because that is not what it is. Speech is other than itself because of what it is. Altizer says that speech must always be moving. "Only by being against itself can speech be for itself, and only by negating itself can speech continue to speak."[17] Theology cannot take possession of an original text, because in the beginning there is silence. The simple identities of the silence cannot be spoken, because the speaking is a re-presentation that is a difference. Theology, including Altizer's, moves, must move, in this dialectic of speech and silence, presence and absence. Theological thinking is a theater of representations, a theater of difference, and its textuality is a montage. A tight system of theology is only a well-ordered montage. Theological argumentation is a display and a forgetfulness. When the seams are too closely aligned the God of the gaps disappears, and theology is victimized by the illusion of literalism.

Altizer seldom makes this mistake: he uses language to violate language. In his speech we hear a deep resonance with the identity of speech. Not only does he allow the seams in his theological montage to show, but also what some readers might react to as a seaminess in his theology is his continual recognition of the necessary dialectic between speech and silence. Just as Freud followed lines of resistance to gain access to the unconscious, Altizer follows the seams to maintain access to silence. The seams sometimes gape when language is troped or negated in the achievement of speech. The appearance of a gap can reveal language as it is in the otherness of its material difference from a simple identity that now appears as silence. That is, language appears as language. There is no authentic text behind the given text. There is silence. Every textual dissemination is the creation of difference that is also an otherness.

Altizer sees very clearly that because we have named God we are an exilic people. We cannot now go behind the act of naming to a paradise of possibilities. "Yet the name of God makes exile manifest in its source, and thereby in its finality, a once and for all finality eradicating every possibility of the nonbeginning of actuality."[18] The actualization in speech gives a location, a regional presence that differs and defers from the omnipresence or total presence of God. The unknown God of total presence differs from the known God of our naming. The unspeakable name of God obviously cannot be spoken. But we have spoken the name of God, which is not a knowledge of the unspeakable name of God. It is not simply that we have spoken the name of God and should remedy our exilic condition by withdrawing from further speech. We have spoken and we are speaking. The name of God has an identity through difference in the order of meaning. Meaning is afflicted by the name of God.

The birth of the identity that is other than itself has already occurred. Abortion is too late. Through speech we have come to dwell in the order of language, the realm of meaning. It is through speech that speech must violate itself, continue to move, and move by continually deconstructing its achievement.

Altizer speaks to the name of God by hearing Nietzsche's prophet come down from the mountain and declare that God is dead, and by hearing the Christian proclamation of the death of God through the crucifixion of the fully incarnate Christ. The death of God is the grand trope that reveals the seamy side of theology in all of Altizer's books. The death of God is a profound *No saying* to the name of God, and this *No saying* permeates Altizer's work as it issues forth in an eschatological and apocalyptic *Yes.*

The trope of the death of God shifts the meaning of consciousness. Consciousness is what it is, both distancing and differentiating, only if it never fulfills itself as total consciousness. The death of God empties the name of God of any promise or power of subsuming the fractured particularities of experience into the wholeness of a total presence. The name of God is a sign that can only signify a concept of God that is other than God. Altizer is not making a statement about God when he talks about naming God, except when marking an absence. He is making a statement about speech and consciousness.

To continue to think theologically and recognize Altizer's insights into speech, we must develop a speech that has itself been transformed by the grand trope of the death of God. What is needed is a new mode of religious understanding, a genre to embody eschatological thinking. As early as his book on Eliade, Altizer claims the first requirement in a quest for a new mode of religious understanding is a confession of the death of God of Christendom.[19] In this study the claim seems to be more a statement of the exhaustion of Christendom than a statement about the good news of the death of God in a kenotic Christology. In *The Gospel of Christian Atheism* the death of God is an actual and real event. It is an event he claims happened in a cosmic and historical sense.[20] This is a claim that God died in Christ and is not the more common acknowledgment of an eclipse of God in secular consciousness. "Yes, God dies in the Crucifixion: therein he fulfills the movement of the Incarnation by totally emptying himself of his primordial sacrality."[21] This death transforms transcendence into immanence. The way of transcendence is reversed. In *The Descent into Hell* the negation of God is the realization of faith. This again is a Christian claim. "Certainly, the death of God is a Christian symbol, pointing to the center of what the Christian has always known as the passion of Christ."[22] Consciousness is shifted. Individual identity perishes in the "night brought on by the death of God."[23] What first appeared as an assessment of our time becomes a doctrinal affirmation of cosmic significance that deeply alters our understanding of consciousness and speech. In fact, it is sometimes difficult for the reader to reconcile the altered understanding of consciousness and speech with the prior affirmation of the cosmic significance of the death of God in Christ. Altered consciousness turns back on itself and metaphorizes the origin of its metaphoricity. If this happens, a cosmic literalism is as questionable as a historical literalism.

It is not as if we ever knew a time of simple identities. We were born into speech. We were born into exile. We were born after the death of God.

If there is one clear portal to the twentieth century, it is a passage through the death of God, the collapse of any meaning or reality lying beyond the newly discovered radical immanence of modern man, an immanence dissolving even the memory of the shadow of transcendence.[24]

Thus it is within the boundaries of our radical immanence that we will be restricted in understanding the cosmic significance of Altizer's Christ.

Altizer clearly distinguishes the eschatological Christ from the Christ of Christendom. This distinction helps remove familiar expectations that hinder understanding of the cosmic significance of the eschatological Christ within the boundaries of radical immanence. According to Altizer, the familiar orthodox and Catholic formulations of Christian doctrine result from a process of de-eschatologizing the original faith of Christianity.[25] The redemption of the profane world in the proclamation of the kingdom of God was so radically separated from the idea of the Christ that the proclamation of Jesus was nullified in the proclamation that Jesus is the Christ. A noneschatological notion of redemption "necessitated a new idea of Christ: the Messiah—Son of Man, whom the early church had proclaimed, and whose coming marked the advent of the end of the world, now became the Logos Christ in whose image the world had been made."[26] Altizer marks this as "the path by which Christianity reversed and negated its eschatological ground, and gradually but ever more comprehensively evolved into the opposite of its original faith and vision."[27] Jesus becomes the cosmic lord and transcendent redeemer[28] and the body of Christ becomes the church.[29]

Redemption through the body of Christ is now separated from the body of humanity. The reversal in the transcendent domain that is the meaning of radical immanence was reversed. An absolute religion evolves that is far from what we experience within the domain of our radical immanence. The radical theologian recognized that the reestablishment of an absolute religion negates the meaning of the incarnation. The world is denied the redemptive presence of the kenotic Christ and is given in return only a trace of the absent Christ that is Wholly Other. It is the vision of Christianity as an absolute religion that radical theology rejects.

In contrast, "by coming to know the *total* presence of God in the Incarnation, Blake and every radical Christian is liberated from the God who is Wholly Other than man...."[30] The heteronomous law of

absolute religion pales next to the claims of experience when the
Wholly Other is emptied into a radical immanence. For Blake and for
Altizer, the incarnation is a fall into *experience.* This is part of the
redemptive meaning of radical immanence. It is a part of what Altizer
means when he uses the term *kenosis.* We experience the kenotic
Christ in Jesus' proclamation of the presence of the kingdom of God.
This proclamation is an eschatological epiphany. Its experiential time
is always "here and now." Christendom has reversed the reversal of
eschatological faith and clings to the familiar name of God. "It is
precisely a bondage to former revelation, or to preeschatological
epiphanies of God, which is the deepest barrier to an acceptance of
the actual presence of the Kingdom of God."[31]

Altizer does formulate a Christology that confronts the incompati-
bility between the incarnate Christ and the primordial Christian God.[32]
Prior to *Total Presence,* which is representative of a new genre for
theological thinking first seen in *The Self-Embodiment of God,* the
clearest statements of his Christology are in *The Gospel of Christian
Atheism* and in *The Descent into Hell.* In these two books this
Christology is compared and contrasted with traditional formulations.
Both books affirm the centrality, the reality, and the cosmic importance
of the eschatological proclamation of the kenotic Christ. Not only is
Altizer's theology specifically Christian, but it is so thoroughly per-
meated by the incarnational motif that even unsympathetic Christian
readers are here confronted by the scandal of their own faith. Altizer
is part of that theological company that insistently bears witness to
the incarnation. His Christology is not a philosophical theory about
the Christ-event as much as it is a close reading of the text and a
careful listening to the language and proclamation of Jesus. In fact,
the proclamation of the presence of the kingdom of God shapes his
basic philosophical posture. The eschatological gospel is a radical
reversal of religious consciousness.

He is not talking about the discovery of an eternal truth. The
incarnation is the actualization of a presence that alters the meaning
of consciousness, the meaning of world, and the meaning of humanity.
It has to do with all that we mean by the world of the flesh. It is here
that the power of the Word of God has a meaningful reference.

"The Christian Word appears in neither a primordial nor eternal
form: for it is an incarnate Word, a Word that is real only to the
extent that it becomes one with human flesh."[33] The only access we
have to the Word is through the oneness with human flesh. This is

not a speculative metaphysical claim. It is within the dynamics of actual experience that the Word has its significance.

Jesus proclaims a kingdom dawning at the center of life and the world.[34] The kingdom of God is not otherworldly, although it is also a negation of the world, making it other than what it is. An affirmation of total immanence combined with the apocalyptic closure of worldly hopes describes the authentic situation of the Christian—hardly a description of Christendom as we have known it. This is a refusal to resurrect the primordial transcendent God. The meaning of the dawning of the kingdom of God is the total reversal of worldly conditions and the denial of an extraworldly transcendence. The "affairs of the world are completely irrelevant, for the total end is immediately at hand."[35] This is what it means to affirm with Altizer the scholarly judgment "that the symbolic center of Jesus' proclamation is the apocalyptic symbol of the Kingdom of God."[36] In an eschatological faith the form of this world is passing away, including the network of relationships that constitutes the meaning of naming the primordial God.

We have to talk about the transcendence and immanence of God in a new way. By the time of *Total Presence* Altizer has developed a new genre for talking about God, but in *The Descent into Hell* he continues to carry his inquiry through the transgressive force of the question. He asks,

> Is it possible to understand pure transcendence as a symbolic image of the primordial God and pure immanence as a symbolic image of the Kingdom of God.... Is it possible to conceive the possibility of an eschatological movement from transcendence to immanence, a total movement whereby the fullness of transcendence passes into a final immanence?[37]

The emphasis on a *final* immanence prevents the incarnation from being understood as an interesting but transitory interlude within history. The apocalyptic symbol of the kingdom of God brings an end to history as the dominant symbol of the human condition. It is indeed a strange form of faith that transforms the proclaimer into the proclaimed and ignores the original proclamation. Altizer's unwillingness to be deaf to the apocalyptic proclamation is the shaping force of the eschatological faith he spreads before his reader even if his formulations reverse all previous images of God.

> Most deeply of all, it [the dawning of the Kingdom] shatters the images

of the transcendence and the mystery of God, and not only shatters but reverses them: for here the mystery of God comes to bear the opposite of its original and given meaning.[38]

"Yes, we must also come to see that there can be no real *parousia* of God, no real final and total presence of God, apart from a negation of every other presence and identity of God."[39]

A rigorous reading of the kenotic transformation of radical transcendence into radical immanence prepares us for the most complex reversal of ordinary Christian consciousness. What does it mean to talk about the resurrection of Christ after the death of God? Ascension into an otherworldly primordial transcendence would abrogate the meaning of the incarnation. The final meaning of God has emptied and negated all former meanings. The resurrection must be consistent with the final meaning, or else the resurrection negates the proclamation of Jesus.

"Let us be fully aware that if we are to arrive at a truly eschatological understanding of resurrection, then we must be prepared to negate and annul the ancient mythical meaning of resurrection."[40] The trajectory of the incarnation has been along the lines of a descent. It is through images of descent and humiliation that Altizer envisions the consummation of the incarnation that is also the resurrection.[41] "Symbolically speaking, this is no more and no less than a means of understanding or envisioning the resurrection of Christ as the descent into Hell."[42]

Jesus initiates a new age, and this is the new age of eternal death not eternal life. This is the most radical and far-reaching claim of a kenotic Christology. It is a consistent consummation of the incarnation.

> What dies in Jesus is the transcendent form of Spirit, and what is resurrected in Jesus is a new and final mode of flesh. From this point of view, it is of vital importance, symbolically, to apprehend the passion and death of Jesus as culminating not in eternal life or Heaven but rather in an eternal death or Hell.[43]

He characterizes Jesus as "the man of Hell" who actualized eternal death, a death embodying the death of eternal life.[44] This is a vision that is not simply forced on us by the logic of the totality of the incarnation, but is celebrated by Altizer as the actualization of the eternity and bliss of heaven in the finality and immediacy of death. In the finality of death the inevitability of death as inscribed in the human condition becomes identified with the innermost goal of the kingdom of God.[45]

Transcendence is regionalized within a radical immanence, within the boundaries of the human condition. Liberation and redemption must find their locus within a radical immanence. This requires a new form of humanity, and it is this new form of humanity that Altizer proclaims as the good news. The distance between God and humanity is dissolved and both are transformed. His proclamation is a consent to this reality as he sees it in the witness to the incarnation; it also is witnessed in the revolutionary twentieth-century voices of art, music, and literature. For many of his readers, Altizer's work will be a resonating consent to experience and not a celebration of that experience.

It is when we ask how the historical Jesus can be the contemporary Christ that we see the implications of the incarnation or death of God for life as it is lived. The death of God is experientially known as the surrender of autonomous individual consciousness:

> It is that form of consciousness and selfhood which is enclosed within itself, or isolated and apart by virtue of its own autonomy, which collapses as a consequence of the advent of the death of God. . . . The night brought on by the death of God is a night in which every individual identity perishes.[46]

The eternal death of Jesus is the closure of all enduring individual identities.

Radical immanence is the meaning of a kenotic Christology, but it is also the witness of twentieth-century culture to the human condition. We are not able to live centered outside the contingencies and vicissitudes of time.[47] With the death of God we have lost the eternity of selfhood and thus its autonomy from history. The death of God gives us a knowledge of the darkness, not so we can dispel the darkness but so we can begin to see darkly. "By knowing that our darkness and emptiness are reflections or images of the dissolution of the transcendence and sovereignty of God, we can be open to the death or end of a divine transcendence and sovereignty as the way to our eternal death."[48] Even if the secular reader were to remain unconvinced by Altizer's Christianity, Altizer's theological articulations and imaginative display of what it means to be a being-towards-death are not easy to set aside. What sometimes appears to be a call to madness and death must be balanced in our evaluative judgment with what it means to consent to reality. Even the social revolutions of our century have brought an end to the illusion of integral and intrinsic human identity.[49] How can we now thematize and articulate what it means to be human?

Altizer brings us to the awareness of a series of refusals and recognitions. His beginnings seem obvious: We must not speak the unspeakable. We must not name the unnameable. But his refusals reach much further and generally reject the great clichés of Western metaphysics and its attendant theologies. His recognitions are almost always reversals. Enlightenment is consummated in darkness. The resurrection confirms the new age of eternal death. The way up becomes the way down. The ascent into heaven is a descent into hell.

These refusals and recognitions are dialectical, and implied in this dialectic is what I consider to be the most important recognition by Altizer and about Altizer: the literal language of consciousness is a metaphor of the real. It is this insight that allows him to develop a theological literalism rejecting metaphorical and allegorical interpretation without sacrificing the postcritical intelligibility of his work. He has mastered the metaphoricity of the work as a whole, in contrast to those who work with metaphors.

Nowhere in his work is this more clearly achieved than in *Total Presence* and *The Self-Embodiment of God.* In both books he works within the immediate arena of speech actualizing a meaning that is present to this speech. The themes of his earlier books resonate with the metaphorical achievement of literal proclamation in these books. What is different is that there seems to be a genuine effacement of the subject. The works do not display the interior of the artist or theologian but rather turn toward the fullness of language.

In *Total Presence* our attention is drawn to the parabolic language of Jesus and the poetic voice that resides in the language of today. But it is not a study of the language of Jesus or of poetry. It is a reading of the parabolic and poetic voice and is itself that voice. Altizer is a reader of culture, and this reading is an achievement with its own voice. He sees that "voice itself is praxis, the praxis of a world come of age."[50] The fully parabolic speech of Jesus embodies and evokes an actuality that is present and immediate. It is praxis. "Indeed, it is the negation, transcendence or reversal of vision itself, a negation of all horizons and planes lying outside of and beyond the pure immediacy of speech."[51] In modern poetic language "the true poetic voice ceases to be a unique and individual voice and becomes a voice transcending any possible individual ground or source."[52] There is no center of identity, no God, no individual identity that gives meaning to what is present. What is present is finally and totally present.

Altizer's theology is still a theology of radical negation, because it is only by way of a negative assault on all established forms of identity through the language of Jesus or the language of today that a total and final presence manifests itself. Total presence marks a day of judgment and dissolution. It is an apocalypse now. It is also good news. The surface sham of the audible and visible humanity of mass society and mass culture is unmasked. Altizer draws us toward his understanding of a universal and common humanity that is not simply identified with the sense of humanity that is at hand in the social, religious, and political institutions that hedge in our lives. He is also wise enough to know that true revolution is more than an assault on visible institutions. "Only by going beyond our own interior can we reach those deep crevices leading to a truly common and universal humanity."[53] Redemption has a real and realizable meaning for Altizer—the giving of ourselves over to our common and universal humanity. There is an ascetic fulfillment to Altizer's theology. He concludes *Total Presence* by writing, "Not only is the only true paradise the paradise that we have lost, but the only regained paradise is the final loss of paradise itself."[54]

He cannot name the universal and common humanity any more than he can name God. We have no place to stand that is not in the middle of experience. It is to the dialectic of speech and silence, presence and absence, that we again return. We experience a new anonymity that is also a fullness. Altizer illustrates this point with a reference to Far Eastern landscape paintings where we cannot easily identify the human presences they might contain. "Soon we realize that these presences are enriched by their apparent absence and that our inability to see a singularly human form is precisely what makes possible our ability to see the fullness of a human identity which otherwise is invisible to us."[55]

Theological thinking is not only challenged but is transformed by the radical vision of Altizer. He, like a landscape painter, has enriched the presence and meaning of God and our common humanity by portraying their apparent absence. He has contributed to our inability to see integral and unique forms, which in turn has contributed to our ability to see a final and total presence.

NOTES

1. Thomas J. J. Altizer, *The Self-Embodiment of God* (New York: Harper & Row, 1977), 1.

2. Thomas J. J. Altizer, *Mircea Eliade and the Dialectic of the Sacred* (Westport, Conn.: Greenwood Press, 1975 [1963]), 65–66.

3. Ibid., 79.

4. Thomas J. J. Altizer, *The Gospel of Christian Atheism* (Philadelphia: Westminster Press, 1966), 18.

5. Ibid., 76.

6. Thomas J. J. Altizer, *The New Apocalypse: The Radical Christian Vision of William Blake* (Lansing, Mich.: Michigan State Univ. Press, 1967), 85.

7. Thomas J. J. Altizer, *The Descent Into Hell: A Study of the Radical Reversal of the Christian Consciousness* (New York: Seabury Press, 1979 [1970]), 34.

8. Ibid., 7.

9. Ibid., 91.

10. Altizer, *Self-Embodiment of God,* 3.

11. Ibid., 5.

12. Ibid., 55.

13. Ibid., 65.

14. Ibid., 37.

15. Ibid., 17.

16. Ibid., 21.

17. Ibid.

18. Ibid., 29.

19. Altizer, *Mircea Eliade,* 13.

20. Altizer, *Gospel of Christian Atheism,* 103.

21. Ibid., 113.

22. Altizer, *Descent Into Hell,* 58.

23. Ibid., 153.

24. Altizer, *Gospel of Christian Atheism,* 22.

25. Altizer, *Mircea Eliade,* 68.

26. Ibid., 71.

27. Altizer, *Descent Into Hell,* 105.

28. Altizer, *New Apocalypse,* 132.

29. Altizer, *Gospel of Christian Atheism,* 132.

30. Altizer, *New Apocalypse,* 106.

31. Thomas J. J. Altizer, *Total Presence: The Language of Jesus and the Language of Today* (New York: Seabury Press, 1980), 50.

32. Altizer, *Gospel of Christian Atheism,* 43.

33. Ibid., 40.

34. Altizer, *Descent Into Hell,* 103.

35. Ibid., 73.

36. Ibid., 71.

37. Ibid., 86–87.

38. Ibid., 101.

39. Altizer, *Total Presence,* 49.

40. Altizer, *Descent Into Hell,* 116.

41. Ibid., 118.
42. Ibid., 119.
43. Ibid., 126.
44. Ibid., 127.
45. Cf. ibid., 131.
46. Ibid., 153.
47. Ibid., 159.
48. Ibid., 161.
49. Altizer, *Total Presence,* 83.
50. Ibid., 7.
51. Ibid., 11.
52. Ibid., 80.
53. Ibid., 104.
54. Ibid., 108.
55. Ibid., 30.

Index

Church, 87, 115
Coagulation, 21–22
Cogito, 34
Collection, 26, 30
Communication, 27
Condensation, 21–23, 26, 29
Conscience, intellectual, viii, ix
Consciousness, viii, 5, 10–11, 13–
    14, 19–20, 22–30, 34, 36, 38,
    40, 45, 59–60, 64–65, 100,
    109, 113–114, 119
Contingency, 87
Construction, 46, 73, 75–77, 79, 86,
    93, 102–3
Contrast, 27, 29–30, 33
Critique, 34, 82
    second order, ix
    transcendental, vii
Critique of Pure Reason, viii
Crossan, John Dominic, 92
Culture, 39, 65, 74, 97, 101
    secular, 87

Darkness, 1, 11, 13, 16, 19–20, 25,
    27, 38, 45–46, 89, 105, 108,
    119
Death, eternal, 118–20
Death of God, 19, 74–75, 92, 106,
    108, 110, 113–15, 119
Deconstruction, ix, 36, 41, 46, 72–
    73, 75, 78–79, 82, 92–94, 103
Defamiliarization, 105
Defense, 65
Deferral, 66, 80, 83, 97, 102–3
Denial, 46
Depth, 26, 73
Derrida, Jacques, 37, 39–40, 57, 71,
    111
Descartes, Rene, 32, 34
Descent, 25
Descent into Hell, 110, 114, 116–
    17
Desire, viii, 3, 12–13, 21, 32, 44,
    80, 100–103, 105–6, 108
Despair, 34

Diachronic, 35–37, 77
Dialectic, 54, 56, 65, 68, 71, 76, 79,
    91, 100, 103, 109, 112–13,
    120–21
Différance, 111
Difference, 25, 50, 57, 64, 66, 72,
    83, 97–99, 111–13
Dionysus, 16
Discourse, 2, 5–7, 9–11, 16–17,
    27–28, 33, 38, 43, 64, 72, 74,
    78–79, 86, 97
    mixed, 38, 41–43, 45–46, 67,
    71–72, 77
Discursive situation, 5, 9
Disguise, 13, 22, 24, 27, 64, 74
Displacement, 15, 21–24, 26–29,
    41, 44, 64, 83, 111
Dissemination, 59, 65, 71, 85, 93,
    113
Distance, 5
Distortion, 64
Drama, public, 83–84
    social, 82, 84–85
Dream, 20–22, 24–25, 33, 39, 42,
    64
Dream-work, 20–27, 29
Dualism, 36
Duplicity, 9, 22, 70, 77, 100
Dwelling, ix

Ebeling, Gerhard, 15
Economics of force, 35–36, 38, 51–
    52, 57, 68, 70, 73, 79, 90, 101
Economy, physiological, 68
Ecstacy, 46
Effacement, 40, 53
Ego, 16
    imaginal, 38
Eliade, Mircea, 109, 114
Ellis, Havelock, 25
Empiricism, 4, 33
Enigma, 20, 68, 87
Enlightenment, viii, 77, 86, 89
Epiphanies of darkness, viii, ix, x
Epiphora, 43–44